TO J
JAN E

BEST WISHES

Doug

From Here to There on

18 Wheels

(Mostly)

A Collection of Trucking Tales

BY B.D. FIRTH

Illustrated by Kevin Docherty

Produced by:

FriesenPress
Suite 300 – 852 Fort Street
Victoria, BC, Canada V8W 1H8

www.friesenpress.com

Distributed to the trade by The Ingram Book Company

Table of Contents

To my mother, Eleanor Marie Firth, author —who taught me the love of words by example

To my children Mike, Cathy and Pat, who share many of my trucking memories

To my wife, Brenda, who encouraged me to write it all down

To my trucking family: the dispatchers and fellow drivers, without whose interaction the stories could not have happened.

This book is a compilation of the sometimes unusual or funny situations in the wild and wonderful trucking life of Benjamin Douglas Firth.

All items are true and have been lived by the author. Names, at times, have been changed as well as some dates, due to the old man's memory, or lack of same.

I hope you get good feelings out of this publication, or at least a smile or two.

From Here to There on

18 Wheels

(Mostly)

A Collection of Trucking Tales

Chapter 1

In the Beginning

When I was just a kid in the process of growing up, all of the
other kids had dreams and aspirations of what they wanted to

be when they grew up. The girls wanted to be nurses, teachers or, of course, mothers and most of the boys dreamed of being a policeman, a fireman or the pilot on a plane. In my case, I was always fascinated by the trucks going up and down the road, hauling every kind of stuff you could think of. It took a lot of years and a lot of different jobs to realize my secret ambition of owning my own truck. It was my idea of a white knight on his mighty steed, trekking up and down the road doing good deeds, etc.

The first driving job I had was as an ice man at Garvin's Ice & Fuel in Langley, piloting a little one-ton truck. This hardly qualified as any kind of knight but it was a step in the learning process. Over the years, as my experience grew, so did the size of the trucks and the loads. Finally, after several years of driving for other people and driving pieces of junk that had to be repaired before you got a mile out of town, I ordered a truck of my own.

After making arrangements to buy the truck, I went to several different trucking companies to check out which company had the latest equipment and the industry reputation that stood out among the others. I signed on with my number-one choice, then gathered the gear I needed: tarps, chains, belts, etc. After several months waiting, I finally had my red and yellow cab-over dream.

My first run was empty to Squamish where I picked up a load of lumber for the docks. It was not a very auspicious start, but I just put it down to breaking in. When I arrived back in the yard, I got a load to Ashcroft and a back haul from Merritt. I thought this was better; but the scuttlebutt I heard from other drivers was that everyone was having a big laugh at my expense. In the industry, everyone considered back and forth from Ashcroft and Merritt as the dregs of assignments. When I had put up with these loads for five trips, I asked one of the other drivers why I was getting the crap loads. His answer was to ask me how much booze I was giving the dispatchers for my loads. He told me two bottles would get me a good load, maybe California, and a case of beer was good for a Prince George run.

When I heard this I realized I still had a lot to learn. I took my bills of lading for Ashcroft, stomped into the office of the guy who had hired me, and told him, "I quit!" When he asked me why, I threw the bills of lading on his desk and told him. He claimed he knew nothing of this, but asked me to follow him. We went down to dispatch and he asked the fellow there, "What have we got for California?" The guy answered, "Two loads for Fred, one after the other." The boss said, "Send Fred to Ashcroft. Doug has those two loads to California and no more B.S." The dispatchers were not very happy, but after that I got the loads and it was done fairly.

This was the beginning of a long and happy relationship with this red and yellow company. We had our moments—some good, others not so good—as you will see from some of the anecdotes in this book. I also hope you will get some laughs, smiles and moments of wonder. I know the stories are true, because I lived them during the many years I was a lease operator for Arrow Transfer (now called Arrow Transportation Services). Being a lease "op" required you to supply the tractor, and the company (Arrow) to supply the trailer and the load.

The Bear Facts

 Sometimes, as in this case, you went with an empty trailer to pick up a customer's load for delivery. This particular assignment was destined for Seattle, Washington. Two trucks were sent to Great Bear Mine, north of Hyder, Alaska, to pick up a large generator. I was driving my truck while the other rig was owned and driven by Jack McDonald. Jack was a little guy who hardly looked old enough to have a license, but he was a good driver and a good friend.

To get to our destination, we had to turn left at Prince George, drive to Hazelton, and turn right toward Meziadin Junction, which allows you the option of turning right toward Cassiar or left toward Stewart. The roads had been very rough since we left the highway but as we turned toward Stewart the road became a little better. A big sign came into view and it warned: Watch for Ice on Road. As we chatted on our radios, we laughed about the sign, since it was the middle of summer. Jack was leading and as he went around a corner, he called me on the C.B. and said, "Take it easy, there really IS ice on the road . . . chunks of it!"

As I came around that corner there were a half-dozen blocks of ice on the road and when we looked to the left, we saw part of Bear Glacier up on the hill. Beside the road was a lake and the ice had fallen off the glacier, come down and floated across the lake and finally landed on the road. After we edged our way through this peculiar roadblock, we carried on to Stewart. Stewart is one of B.C.'s seaports and lies about a mile from Hyder, Alaska. The town of Hyder consists of one small confectionary that sells souvenirs and trinkets, and four saloons. The store in owned by the U.S. customs officer and usually sports a "Gone Fishing" sign, as does the customs office. The saloons are a little different, too. Three of them are open 23 hours a day . . . and one is open for one hour a day. As you can probably guess, the main occupations are drinking and fishing.

They also have a golf course, whose name is self-explanatory. It's the "Low Tide Golf and Country Club." It lies on a 30-foot wide strip of sand that's available whenever the tide is out. It starts in Hyder and it runs to Stewart: one hole!

After passing the "Gone Fishing" sign, we found ourselves in Alaska and we picked up our bottle of Ever-clear (Alaska's national drink, 190 proof)—strictly for medicinal purposes, of course, or if you have to do a stay-over for a week. On Everclear, driving is out of the question: you are barely able to walk and wake up with the hangover to end all hangovers. We found out the food source in town was the Seven Seas Pub, so we stopped for lunch and then headed up to the mine. This stretch is 18 miles of the most beautiful scenery in the world. The road runs in and out of Alaska eight times in eight miles. The Bear Glacier runs alongside the road, or rather 500 to 1,000 feet below the left side of the road for all of those miles. It is a gorgeous shade of blue, unlike anything I have ever seen. After eight miles the glacier turns left, sort of like a boomerang, and heads up the mountain for another ten miles. When

I had completed that drive, on this narrow twisting road from Perdition, I drew my first breath in about an hour.

Near the top of the mountain, past more of that beautiful scenery, we arrived at the mine camp and parked. Then we were told we had a two-day minimum wait because the parts we were hauling were worth several million dollars and had to be packed in crates made from 12 by 12 timbers, bolted to the trailer and packed with layers of rubber.

We were shown to our rooms and the showers. After we showered, we went to the cookhouse for dinner and as soon as the meal was over, everyone took their chairs outside, leaned against the building and just stared at the scenery as the glacier came right up to the camp. Sitting there, we noticed cars and trucks going into a tunnel in the glacier, so we asked about it. We were told we weren't actually at the mine yet; it was nine miles away, on the other side of the ice. There was a 30-foot wide tunnel through to the mine that we still had to navigate. The ice with the headlights glowing through it was magnificent, more beautiful than you can imagine.

We spent the next two days playing pool and ping pong, reading, sleeping and generally trying to amuse ourselves, but eventually we became bored. In desperation, we spoke to the foreman about alternate diversion and he said we could take his pick-up, if we liked, and head down to the dump where there was a mama grizzly parked at the bottom with her two cubs. We got directions, grabbed his keys and away we went on Jack and Doug's Magnificent Adventure.

When we arrived at the dumpsite, I parked about 20 feet from the edge of an approximately 20-foot drop to the dump. We cautiously neared the edge and as we did, we saw the sow and the cubs down at the bottom of a steep bank. Then the sow saw us! She started to growl and headed up the bank with garbage flying everywhere. We stood there for a minute, petrified with fear, and then we both took off running. Keeping in mind that Jack was all of 140 pounds and I was tipping the scales at 275, at the initial blast off, I thought I was bear breakfast. It took about 20 feet for me to catch up and pass Jack, about the same time as we both flew right past the truck. We were not about to stop for anything! The look on Jack's face as I passed him, flying, said it all: "Oh, shit! I'm bear food." Up to then I guess he'd thought that if the bear was going to snack on anyone, it would be the big guy.

Just then I realized I could hear laughter—gales of laughter. It was the shop foreman and five or six mechanics, just about rolling on the ground, laughing. When he sent us down, he knew the bear couldn't make it up the hill, so he loaded the shop guys into another pick-up and snuck up as we were walking down to the garbage dump's edge. They had a great laugh and later we all went down and stood there one more time. Even then it still scared the hell out of me!

Chapter 2

Signs of the Times

Check Out Time

Not many of my driving assignments were without incident and these days, as I look back on these adventures, it brings a smile to my face and warms a special place in my heart. I really miss driving and I enjoy reliving the events, the exploits and the escapades; some were humorous, some scary, but all were part of my life as a long-haul trucker.

I recall one incident that happened fairly close to home. I had just finished buying a new truck with all the bells and whistles, and because of the new truck Arrow gave me a brand-new trailer to use on my first trip. The first load was to go empty to Squamish and pick up a load of lumber to go to Surrey Fraser Dock. When I approached the scales where the road forks toward Horseshoe Bay and Squamish, the sign on the scales read "Check brakes,"—so I pulled in and stepped on the tractor brakes and pulled the handle on the trailer brakes. They all locked up great as they were brand new.

As I pulled out and turned toward Squamish, a guy stepped out from under the overpass and walked up to my side of the cab. He asked for my registration and insurance. I said, "What's the problem?" and he said it was that I didn't stop and check my brakes and he started to write me a ticket. I said, "First of all, this is a brand new truck and trailer; secondly, the sign says "Check brakes," not *stop* and check brakes. Then I asked why they were being so particular and he said, "Because there have been three deaths on the road going down to Horseshoe Bay; and besides, you're supposed to obey the rules."

I said, "The sign reads "Check brakes" and I did that, therefore you have no legal right to stop me. Also, I'm going to Squamish, not Horseshoe Bay, and you can keep your ticket. I'm not paying." Nonetheless, he insisted that I take the ticket and when I took it, I told him I would see him in court, as there was no way he could charge me for a law that didn't exist. I actually did send the ticket in, with the fee, stating I would appear to dispute the charge. About a week later, I got a letter from the police department with my payment returned, saying that the police had decided not to pursue the matter at this time. The next time I went by those scales, there were four new signs up that all said "Stop and Check Brakes!"

The Law Works in Mysterious Ways

A truck driver was pulled over by an RCMP. The officer told him to get out of the truck, and noticed that the driver appeared to be putting something in his mouth as he stepped out of the cab. Figuring that the driver was putting away his pep pills, the Mountie asked, "Did I just see you swallow something?"

"Yep, that was my birth control pill," said the driver.

"Birth control pill?" asked the RCMP officer.

"Yep, soon as I saw your lights flashing, I knew I was going to get screwed!"

What Hit the Fan?

Shortly after buying my new truck, I received a recall notice that the fan on the radiator, which was gear-driven, had to be serviced. I took it to the dealer and had it fixed; it took two days and I lost another load. Once the truck was mobile, my son Pat and I took off with a load of machinery to Prince George. When we passed Williams Lake, the fan came off and went through the radiator. There was no doubt that the mechanic doing the maintenance had never tightened the nut holding the fan.

We checked things out and found that the radiator, the water pump and the fan were shot! I phoned the nearest wrecker and spoke to the owner; as it turned out, he had a tow truck and an auto-wrecking yard. Better still, he had room for us to park and make repairs to our truck in his yard. He showed up a while later with a small tow truck that we didn't think it could move the truck. He figured it out, though: two trips, one for the truck and one for the trailer. The truck was in a spot in his yard that would allow us to work on it. Part of the deal we made was for the use of his homemade crane, which we needed to get the radiator out. After we had it on the ground we saw how many cores were damaged and how bad the fan was.

I put in a call to the dealer who had done the work on the truck and threatened to sue him. He agreed to pay for the damages and to have the parts shipped out as soon as possible. Three days later, there was still no word about any parts already fixed and on their way back, so I began phoning. In the end I waited five full days and then I had to rent a pick-up and go and get the parts myself or wait another three days. When we arrived in Vancouver, nothing was ready and it took another two days to get the parts, then another two days to install them and get the truck running again.

When all is said and done, it was pretty expensive; I was glad it wasn't me that had to pay for it.

Radiator, towing and fan	$ 700.00	Shop & yard rental	450.00
Pick-up Rental	80.00	Gas	65.00 + 30.00 = 95.00
Shipping	110.00	Anti-Freeze	40.00
Crane Rental	300.00	Four nights motel	140.00
Three loads missed (approx.)	1,500.00	**Total**	**$3,415.00**

Made to Order

There are lots of potential problems when you're buying a new truck, especially one that is custom-made one "to order" and engineered by the head office in Kansas City. Everything on the truck was drawn to specifications and approved. To show you how ridiculous this "approval" is, here are some of the screw ups:

The truck was ordered with centre-point steering. This is different from power steering; this type of steering is supposed to work like power steering around town and regular steering on the highway. It didn't work! It took two weeks to get that fixed, which meant two weeks of working time lost.

The truck had two 150-gallon fuel tanks and because they were engineered wrongly, they had to be remounted. Since they were installed too far ahead, the front brakes had to be removed and also the radiator had to be made with an extra row of radiator cores. That meant an extra week of waiting time, plus another week in Montreal because now the radiator would not fit in the truck.

On the way back to Vancouver, the power divider broke down. Then, when I finally got headed home, the transmission overheated—because they had installed the wrong tubing to the transmission oil cooler. When I finally arrived in Vancouver, this brand new engineered truck went straight into the shop and was worked on for four weeks.

Chapter 3

Freaky

Valves a'Poppin'

The high cost of repairs is not the only difficulty truckers run into. Poor strapping and freak accidents can often result in road hazards, as the following memories recall:

The truck was loaded with pallets of pump parts and heading from Alberta to Spokane, Washington. Each pallet had nine valves strapped down on it. The valves were about 60 pounds each and the straps were one-inch metal, tied down with canvas straps.

From Calgary to Osoyoos, they all stayed secure and never moved. As I approached the customs on a small right-hand corner, I heard a scraping noise and when I looked onto the road, I saw one of the pumps passing me. As I saw it go by, I noticed a white Ford Econoline coming and as you can imagine, the pump made a beeline toward the Ford and got it right in the grill. Then it went right through and into the van itself.

I ran over and saw the kid who was at the Ford's wheel. He was a mess . . . that is, he was scared spit-less. He had just turned 16 that day and he was driving his Dad's vehicle; he'd been at it for about three hours. He really was petrified, so I told him to sit tight; the police would be there soon and we would get everything squared away. When the RCMP arrived, we looked at the load to determine where the valve came off the pallet. It was the middle one of the nine valves.

All the valve tie downs were in their original positions; none were loose or broken. Even using a bar, we could not move any of them . . . ten pallets and 90 pieces, and only the one piece had moved! We tried to put it back and even using hammers and bars, there was no way.

At this point I went over and spoke to the kid; he was moaning and groaning and I said, "Are you okay?"

He said, "My dad's going to kill me; it's my first day driving." I assured him that no one could ever, for a second; think what happened was his fault. It was just a fluke accident and if anyone was going to be moaning and groaning, it was me. When I mentioned the kid's situation to the officer, he assured me he would notify the car owner of the freak nature of the accident and the kid would be "off the hook."

Innovation and Duct Tape

Just like life, I've noticed that Canadian, and especially B.C. roads, have lots of twists and turns. In this instance, my load from Arrow was already loaded and tarped. It was a press roll for rolling woodchips into paper and was destined for the Kamloops Pulp Mill. Since the load was tarped when it was first loaded, we did not have much to check, except the tarp straps. We stopped at Cache Creek to eat before we carried on to Kamloops. On the road east, just before you get to Savannah, there is a pretty steep hill that has a sharp right-hand corner.

That area is known as Deadman's Creek. There have been a lot of accidents there; I guess that's the reason for the name.

As I came into the corner, the load shifted to the left and blew two tires off the tractor; I had a huge struggle to stay on the road as the load had moved so much. It pushed us right toward Deadman's Creek, but with much cursing, wrestling with the wheel and keeping the brakes on full, I managed to stop in time to keep us from going over the edge.

When we got out of the truck, we saw that the moron who loaded it didn't chain it down. He just put the load on, threw a tarp over it and left it. The only way we could have seen that was if we'd taken the tarp off, and we hadn't done that because preloads are supposed to be tied down before they're tarped. My partner Pat and I took the tarp off, and after much consideration, took a sledge hammer and a jack and knocked holes in the deck. Then we put the bottom of the jack up against the boards and the other end against the roller, until we could move it enough to tie it down. We re-tarped it and took it very easy the rest of the way to Kamloops, with two flat tires.

We knew this one was a very serious ALMOST!

Hit the Brakes!

During our travels we experienced many odd and unusual events. I think one of the strangest happened one really rainy night when I was coming back to town with a load of lumber. It was a night when it was so black and misty that you could not see the trailer in the mirrors. As I was approaching Abbotsford on the freeway, somebody in a small car pulled up alongside and started honking and blinking his lights. Since I was just getting a run at a small hill, I kept my speed up, but when he became more persistent, I began to ease off on the accelerator. I slowed a bit and pulled off onto the shoulder. As soon as I did, he pulled in front of me and started to stop. I guess no one had ever taught this guy the laws of physics and the fact that it takes a lot longer to stop 84,000 pounds than it does to stop a 2,000-pound car. I hit the brakes and discovered . . . I had none!!

Now, my options were to run right over this guy or swerve back onto the freeway, which was barely visible because of the rain. Without any hesitation, I pulled back onto the four-lane highway and then onto the shoulder. By that time my Jake brake had slowed me down some and I got stopped. If there had been anything on the freeway, there would have been an awful mess.

When the guy finally got to the door of my truck, before he could say a word, I told him that he was lucky to be alive. He hadn't realized that when he saw a set of tandem wheels go flying off my truck and into the Vedder Canal, it meant they'd broken away from the air-line connection to the truck's braking system. Truck brakes are air-driven, so that open air line was no longer pumping air to the other tires. He was trying to do me a favour and he likely did save some lives, although it almost cost him his.

After giving him hell and my sincere thanks, I blocked the airline and chained up the axle, which was scraping on the pavement and sending sparks down the road—one of the things which had further worried the guy. I wonder where I would have ended up without that roundabout warning! So ends another tale of only three wheels on my wagon.

Chapter 4

Road Hazard Game

Some of the worst hazards on the roads are the tourists; the guys pulling the 35 or 40-foot trailers with the underpowered pick-up trucks. I think the second worst are the animals: the moose, deer, elk, caribou and bears. I've had run-ins with all of them at one time or another. One of the most memorable was just south of Prince George, heading toward McBride. It was about three a.m. and I was, along with another truck driven by George, proceeding empty to pick up loads of mining equipment at Tri Cities in Washington State and return it to Dawson Creek. I was in front and undoubtedly breaking the speed limit, when I saw a cow moose come out of a marshy area on my right side. It headed across the road, followed by a yearling calf. As soon as I saw the cow almost across my lane with the calf well behind. I went left to try to make it through between them—but the cow stopped in the middle of the road and instead of going between them, I hit the cow right in the butt. It was like hitting a rock. Two of the feet came up and broke the windshield and the rest came right through the radiator and bent the steering, tearing open the whole front of the truck.

I had both feet braced against the door and I was pulling on the steering wheel with both hands, trying to keep us out of the swamp. Meanwhile, George was busy trying to keep from running into me. Later, he said that all that saved him was seeing the radiator explode. He immediately hit his brakes, landed on my spilled antifreeze and slid sideways almost around my truck. He managed to get stopped without hitting me. There was no sign of the calf, but I'm sure it was all right as it was almost the size of the mother. The mother, however, was beyond help. What we found was barely recognizable as a moose. The truck repair cost just under $9,000 and I lost a week's work plus airfare. The odor never did come out of the truck.

Another time, I was on my way to McKenzie with a load of chlorine on a really black and miserable rainy night. I looked down to check my gauges and as I did, I felt a huge bump. The wheel was almost yanked out of my hands. I stopped the truck and took my flashlight to check things out, but I could find nothing at the front. I looked under the trailer and I found out it was, or had been, a bear; all that was left was one paw. The bear was black and it was really dark so I had missed seeing it. I was lucky to have stayed on the road.

One night I was in the middle of a trip with a brand new truck. I was coming back from Cranbrook, up near Radium Hot Springs, when I met a truck coming the other way. He came on my radio with a warning to watch out for the elk on the left side of the road and said there were five or six of them. I slowed down and kept a close watch on the left side. As I got to the spot he'd warned me about, the elk all came out from the right side of the road. I dodged them the best I could. The road was icy and I had no control. In the middle of the whole thing I heard a couple of small thumps. When I finally got stopped and got out, I noticed that I was missing two lenses from my clearance lights, and after a little searching I turned up two antlers and one road light. I guess when we came together it was just the right amount of force to knock each piece off. The light went back on but there was no hope for the antlers.

On a trip to the Northwest Territories, we ran into a herd of caribou going the same way we were. There were 25 or 30 of them in front of us, all of us heading north. The edges of the road were piled up with snow five or six feet deep. It was all plowed and there was no way for the caribou to get off. They ran in front of us for about ten minutes and we couldn't get them to move off the road. By this time their tongues were hanging out about a foot. We finally came to an opening in the snow and they all got off the road and stood there with their heads down, breathing hard, as we passed them and made tracks for the north country.

On the same trip, when we were running at night with all the lights on, we became a magnet for rabbits or hares. They were attracted to our lights and ran into the front of the truck in such quantities that we had to stop and clean the headlights and the radiator grill. The remains were actually making the truck heat up.

Once, coming back from Roseburg, Oregon, Pat (my son) and I had a load of plywood on for the docks in Vancouver. As we were heading past Eugene, we notice a bunch of birds chasing a flock of small birds. They flew back and forth across the freeway, so close that we could see that the big birds, the ones doing the chasing, were red-tailed hawks. During the pursuit, one of the hawks dove right at us, then pulled away and took another run at us. This time it came straight through the passenger-side windshield and landed in my son's lap: glass and hawk parts all over the place! It took us about two hours to clean it all up and then we had to find a glass shop and get a new windshield put in. Pat was pretty lucky—he only got a few minor cuts.

Around the Cranbrook area, the spring is a really bad time for deer. At night, with your road lights and spotlights on, you can see eyes shining from the fields and the bush everywhere. Most often, the road is covered with dead and crippled animals. When we found injured ones we called the police and they took care of them. On this particular night, one of the deer ran into the side of my truck. Fortunately, it died instantly with no suffering; although it was likely that the survivors suffered. As it was with any animal I hit, it was a very sad thing and since I am a non-hunter, it was also a painful thing for me.

Chapter 5

The Human Element

On the other hand, I'm not always so sensitive about hitting back at humans who try to rope me into things or do me wrong. In most cases I not only get mad; when it's possible, I get even! On one return trip from Roseburg, Oregon, I had full load of plywood going to a lumber business in Burnaby. Before I left Roseburg, I had to tarp the load in case it rained. The load consisted of ten lifts of ¾-inch plywood. I had heard some pretty bad things about the receiver at our destination. He had a habit of saying the top sheet on each lift was ruined by the driver's carelessness and putting a claim in against the driver, who would be charged $800 deductible on the load.

By the time I was unloaded and back at the Arrow office, he had already phoned claiming the damage. When they told me that I had damaged the plywood and it was going to cost me $800, I asked, Where's my plywood?" The Arrow crew told me it didn't work that way, so I asked which of them would pay $800 for nothing.

My next stop was the lumberyard I had delivered to. When the receiver asked what I wanted, I said, "My ten sheets of plywood." He made the mistake of laughing at my request. Then I said if it was damaged, I wanted to see it—and if there was no damage, it was to go back with this load or I would take him out to the parking lot and drive him head-first into the ground and make a bicycle rack out of him.

All of a sudden he came up with the plywood, and a copy of the invoice saying there was no damage. I took the papers in to Arrow and the $800 deductible was all cleared up.

Too bad; he would have made a great bike rack!

The Joker

At one time, I drove for a guy named Ron. This guy was always playing practical jokes. Sometimes they were pretty gross, such as calling you on the CB and telling you that you had a flat tire, or part of your load fell off of the truck, or the road was closed because of an accident. Even after I bought my own truck, he would radio me when I was sleeping telling me that someone was stealing my tires, and I'd have to get out and check it out. I'm sure he had a great time, terrorizing all his drivers.

One night, my son Pat and I were both making the run, and as I was sitting at the truck stop in Hope, Ron got on the radio and asked where I was going. I said I was headed for Trail, and he said he was going to Nelson, and would I wake him up when I got to the turn-off to Trail, where the other direction points to Nelson? I said "sure" and after we had eaten, we took off for the junction. When we got there, Ron's vehicle was parked just off the road at the turnoff. I had this great thought that this was a chance for a bit of revenge.

I had my vehicle creep slowly up to the front of his truck, until the trucks were nose-to-nose, about a foot apart, then signalled Pat to turn on all the lights, road lights and hi-beams. I hit the horns and Ron, who was fast asleep in the seat with his head on the wheel, shot up with a terrified look on his face, his eyeballs as bit as saucers. When I stopped laughing, I pulled alongside him and calmly said, "Awake yet? Just a little practical joke—you know about them, don't you?

Rent to Deliver

Another weird experience involved a load of 60-foot rebar which we had to load on bunks like a logging truck, so when you turn a corner the load actually turns instead of the tires sliding. Getting it loaded took a great deal of messing around with the tying down, flags, long-load signs and lights on the back-end, but we were finally ready. Then we needed to check that the pilot car was on the right radio channel.

It was really awkward getting around corners on surface streets on the way to the freeway. We managed to weave our way around and headed south to Oakland, California. The trip down was a real experience as every scale guy and Highway Patrol Officer between the border and Oakland had to measure the length of the load, check the signs and flags and look at the driver's licence, permits and bills of lading. We must have gone through this about twenty times, and every time they had to check my border crossing card. (This is a card that is approved and checked by the FBI and the CIA to verify that you are of the sterling quality required to set foot on the soil of the good old U.S.A., and not a terrorist or subversive trying to smuggle Canadian rebar into the Holy Land.)

Trials and tribulations notwithstanding, we finally made it to Oakland and after much cursing and backing up and wriggling around corners, we made it to the dock and checked in. We parked about a half-mile down the dock and we untied everything and removed the signs. Then we waited and waited and waited. After two and one-half hours no one had shown up with a crane or a forklift. I finally walked back to the office and was asked by some smart ass why I was still there. I told him how long we had been there and he said, "I know. We were wondering how long you would wait to come and pick up your forklift and unload." I said, "What are you talking about?" and he replied that I would have to rent a forklift and unload my own load.

After several choice comments as to his ancestry and a verbose description of the company, I paid the $75 rental and was informed that when I was finished, all wood and garbage had to be picked up and the lift truck returned. Because the rebar was so long, we should have had two machines, not one, but I wouldn't give him the satisfaction, so we dragged one end of the rebar across the lot because it was too long to lift clear of the blacktop.

When I was finished, the forklift was left where it was with a note to the gentleman snake-oil salesman containing a graphic description of how to commit a biological impossibility on hiself—possibly involving the rebar.

Wilson's Whopper

It's not always the "other guys" who rank zero on the IQ scale, either. While I hate to have to admit it about anybody who could possibly be described as one of our own, some drivers must have been busy on a ten-ten or under the trailer when the common sense was being loaded. A case in point occurred on my return trip from Whitehorse with a load of asbestos for Cassiar, B.C. There was also a second truck on the same run, driven by a guy named Wilson. As we left Cassiar, he was in front, leading the way into a blinding snowstorm. Everything was fine until we came to a steep hill about a half-mile long. There was a mountain up the left side of the road and a drop-off on the right, about 500 feet down to the river at the upper end of the hill, where the road narrowed down to one lane. We came to the hill and I told him on the radio to go ahead and let me know when he was over the top. The reason for this was I had better tires and more power, so I wanted a clear clean run up and over that hill. After several minutes he called and said he was over the top. I started up and I had no trouble until I came to the narrow part of the road. When the road narrowed down, it also turned left. As I came to the turn and the corner, all I could see was the back of his truck, spun out on the ice . . . leaving me nowhere to go.

As soon as I stopped, I started sliding backwards down the hill. All my wheels were sliding on the ice and I tried to steer but the way it was sliding was making steering impossible. As the trailer was heading toward the drop-off, I climbed out and stood on the ladder, trying to steer the back end out onto the road, as it went into a five-foot snow-bank on the edge of the cliff. It suddenly stopped and out I flew, about 15 feet down the road. Fortunately, I only twisted my knee. The tractor sat there, half off the road with the rear of the trailer hanging halfway through a snow-bank and 200 feet above the river.

I got on the radio and asked the idiot, Wilson, what happened. He said after he'd told me it was okay, he spun out. At this point, he really endeared himself to me by announcing that there was no point in him coming back down to try and help me, so he headed for town, with numerous choice words ringing in his ears. About all I could do was put chains on the wheels that I could get to and wait.

After about an hour, a loaded logging truck came down the hill and the driver stopped and said, "It looks like you could use a hand." After I replied with a very loud "YES," we hooked two chains from the back of his truck onto the back of my trailer. I climbed back in the tractor, so I could try to brake if he got me out. As he pulled on the trailer, it popped back onto the road. As the towing was in progress, I looked out the front windows. All I could see was space and the river, way, way down below— because when the driver pulled on the trailer, the tractor followed in the same tracks the trailer had made and ended up hanging in the air over nothing. When it finally hit the road, it was like a cork popping out of a champagne bottle.

I was back to trying to steer and brake as I went backwards down the hill, hooked to the back of a logging truck, which was trying to stay out of my way. My chains were all ripped up from trying to brake. When I finally did stop, it was by running into the back of the load of logs. I hit them so hard, I pushed three logs right up into his cab, so I had to pull them back so he could steer.

I consider myself very fortunate all round. I wasn't hurt badly, my tractor and trailer were fine, my load was okay. Only my chains were shot. The logging truck driver would not take anything for the rescue; he just said, like most drivers up in that country do: "You help somebody else, sometime."

Somewhere, there's guy named Wilson, who doesn't know how lucky he is that I never met up with him again. On the other hand, maybe he does know and that's why I've never seen him.

Don't Yank My Chain

Speaking of chains, this story reminds me of another interesting experience I had on a trip to Prince George one night. My load was a D-8 Cat; as you may realize, a machine this size is very heavy and has to be well chained down. After fastening it down with five nearly new chains, I left Finning Tractor in Vancouver and headed north. By the time I reached the scales in Quesnel I was tired and I decided to sleep for a while, as I only had 75 miles left to Prince George—about two hours. After I had been asleep for about an hour, I heard a noise from outside, like chains clinking. When I look out through the rear-view mirror, I saw a guy with a logging truck taking the chains off of my load. (I should explain here that during the few months prior to this, a lot of drivers had taken to carrying guns with them as there had been many drivers robbed.) I was one of those drivers and when I saw what was happening, I rolled my window down and fired three shots up into the air.

The guy dropped the chains, ran for his truck and took off. When I got out of the truck, the Cat had one chain left on it. The interesting thing was there were five chains left on the ground. All I could figure was that once he had taken my chains, he was going to put them on his chain rack with mine underneath and his covering them up. If I had taken off without those chains on and the load had dropped, I could have killed someone, so I'm glad I ended up with one of his chains. I probably should have shot holes in his truck.

Dry Run

While I'm airing some of my pet peeves—well actually, I have more like a full kennel of grievances—this one will probably hit home to a lot of you readers, especially if you are members of a family. When the White Pass Railroad was on strike and in Whitehorse they were running out of staples, mostly beer, it was our job to keep them supplied. We were loading at Labatt's Brewery, and the guys on forklifts loaded each truck with 24 pallets of beer. I'm not sure but I think each pallet held 444 bottles of beer. Somehow they loaded 25 pallets on my trailer and when I weighed it on the scales in Arrow's yard, I found out I was way overweight. When I took the skid back to the brewery, everybody said I should have taken it home. The thought had entered my mind, but it wasn't the right thing to do.

  When I got back to the brewery, the manager said he had never heard of anybody returning extra beer. He then

asked if I like beer and I said I did. Then he said, "Follow me." He took a pallet and a forklift and walked around to all the different stacks of beer. At every pile he would say, "Do you like this brand?" and when I said "Yes!" he would throw two or three cases onto the pallet. After a while when he came to a stack, he would put on a couple of cases without even asking until there were about 20 cases on the pallet. He took the pallet and put it on top of the load, turned to me and said he seriously doubted that anyone that he knew or that worked for him would have returned that beer. I thanked him very much and headed home. I packed it into the house, and then left for Whitehorse.

I was gone for about a week and on my way home I was thinking about settling back with a cool one. When I arrived, I headed for the fridge; all that was left was one case of dark ale, which I don't like. It appeared my three boys liked all the rest. It doesn't always pay to be honest.

Little bastards!

Chapter 6

A Whiz in the Dark

One night I was headed for Dawson Creek with a load of pipe. When I left home, I headed for the Freeway at 96th Avenue, in Surrey. On my way to the highway, I noticed my brakes were not too good and as there is a wide on-ramp onto the Freeway at 96th, I thought this was a good place to stop and fix them and be out of the way of other traffic. Because there was a slight downhill on the shoulder and I wanted to set up all my brakes, I pulled off onto the shoulder and left my flashers on. When I stopped, I applied my tractor brakes, got out and put large metal corners in front of all the tires (these are triangular-shaped metal pieces to protect the load), and released the tractor brakes. Because all the wheels were blocked, I decided to set them all up at once, this means getting under the truck and adjusting the brakes with a wrench. Then I planned to get back in the truck and apply all the brakes, before picking up the corners.

All of this took place a little before midnight, and the night was as black as the inside of a cat. Working with a flashlight, it took me about 20 minutes. I needed to relieve myself, and because it was so dark I thought I would stand behind the load to do my business. I left my flashlight on the side of the trailer and turned my back to the highway. When I finished, I turned back to the load and it wasn't there! I found out later that the truck and trailer had flattened out those corners and taken off down the freeway. I looked down the road, wondering "What the . . .?" and as I looked, I could see the taillights about a quarter-mile down the road, moving from the right-hand shoulder, across the right lane over to the left lane. Cars and at least one truck passed it. The truck driver told me after, he couldn't figure out what was happening. After about half a mile, the rig went off the left side of the road and into a little ditch. When I got there, the whole thing was upright, all the lights were on and the engine was running. The load never moved and nobody and nothing got hurt or damaged! I called a tow-truck and it cost me $30 to get back on the road.

Ice Dance

When you are travelling in the far north of the Yukon, Northwest Territories and Alaska, there is always something strange and unusual going on around you. If you pay close enough attention, you can see things that are hard to believe.

For example, on one trip we watched three moose being chased down the frozen Stikine River by ten wolves. We sat on the bridge and watched, as it was as comical as Sennett's Keystone Kops at the Buster Keaton festival. First a moose would fall, then half the wolves would go in pursuit, only to slide across the ice past the fallen moose; one moose would get up; then the wolves would fall down; they'd get up and then another moose would slip. Finally, all three of the moose made the shore and the last we saw, the wolves were still trying to get to their feet and follow them. Hopefully, the moose made a clean get-away.

Another oddity in the north is a huge lava field located on both sides of the road along the Nass Valley near the Stikine River in B.C. This phenomenon has obviously been there for many, many years as the lava looks very old. How it got there is the big mystery, though, as there are no mountains around the area.

Sasquatch?

Then there was this one night when my son and I were taking a load to Whitehorse. It had been snowing hard and it let up just as we came to a stretch of road where there had been a forest fire. It had burned everything except a few clumps of green trees. This was just above the Stikine River Bridge, and the road made a bunch of S-turns across the flats. With 18 inches of new powder snow, headlights on high, road lights and spot lights on, it was as bright as day. As we travelled down this leg of winding road, I looked across to the next bend and I saw a tall black figure cross the road. It was still about a hundred yards away and I told my son to shine a spotlight on it. When he did, we could see red eyes flash in the light.

By this time, I had turned the next corner and we could see where it crossed. There were a bunch of green trees about 100 feet from the road and we could still see the eyes shining, about sevenfeet high. When we got to the spot where it had crossed the road, there was a well-defined path in the snow. I stopped and said to Pat, "Grab a flashlight." I grabbed my gun and said, "Come on." We jumped out of the truck and started to walk toward the trees. The first thing that hit us was a horrible smell. Suddenly I turned to Pat and said, "What the hell are we doing?" and with that, we hightailed it back to the truck.

When we got there, the red eyes were still glowing over by the trees, but because of the loose, dry snow, there were no footprints, just a path through it. As we sat in the truck, I said, "That has to be about the dumbest thing I`ve ever done." My son agreed and said, "What were we going to do when we met it? Go the best two out of three, or what?" I said that I was glad we came to our senses and I only wish we had some proof of the happening. This was a brush with the unknown; fortunately, it was not physical.

Making waves!

This is another of the unexplained oddities that happen at times in the wonderful world of trucking. I left Vancouver with a preload of beer to Whitehorse. When I stopped at Cache Creek, I met up with a friend of mine named Klaus who also had a load for Whitehorse, so we decided we would run together. That way, if either of us got into trouble, we would have help and also the conversations we would have on the radio could keep us awake.

The trip up was uneventful and when we were unloaded, we phoned in and were given back hauls to Stewart from Cassiar. The load was asbestos and I did not think much of hauling that, but when it's in a closed trailer, it's not too bad.

Our trip down to Stewart was all right, with no major problems, and just after passing Meziaden Junction, we caught up with two other Arrow drivers with B-trains (double trailers) who were also headed for Stewart with loads of asbestos. Because they were moving pretty good and it wasn't too far to go, we decided to follow them.

We soon came up to Bear Glacier and the first truck rounded the corner above the glacier. Wham! He hit a block of ice that had come through the lake at the bottom of the glacier and had landed on the road. It was the size of a small house and did major damage to the truck. After we looked at his truck, it was pretty obvious that none of us was going anywhere.

We thought that the radio to highway maintenance in Stewart was the best way to go. We all tried and had no luck at all. We couldn't get a signal. I had a new radio with side band (which gets out farther than normal) so I gave it a try. On the second channel I tried, I received an answer. I explained the situation to the guy and asked if he would phone the Highways Department and he said, "Sure." He didn't recognize the phone number, though, and asked where I was. When I explained our location, he said, "I'll be damned! I'm 20 miles out of Nashville, Tennessee."

I said, "You're BS-in' me, are you?"

He said, "No, but sit tight while I phone." I told him to call collect. About five minutes later, he came back on the radio and said the call was done and the Highway Department was on its way. After thanking him profusely, I was about to get his name and phone number when he started to fade out and I lost him.

The Highway trucks showed and after four hours, we were on our way. I tried to reach the ham operator again for several nights in a row and wasn't successful. I finally got home and tried to reach him on my big set—no luck there either. When I contacted the B.C. Highways Department, I finally got his phone number and called him. We spoke for quite a while but neither of us could come up with an answer as to how that original contact had been possible. Weird Science or Calls of the Wild?

Left Turn, Clyde!

A very long load of pipe was to be shipped to Prince George and there had to be two trucks involved, because the pipes were over-length. The loads both had to be loaded on steering trailers, the kind where the trailer is fastened under the back of the load and a second driver rides under the load. The trailer is equipped with a steering wheel, turn signals and a two-way radio to keep in touch so the lead driver can communicate which way to turn and turn back, since the rear driver can't see at all. This was to be a one-day run there and then we could head back.

After spending about three hours getting ready, loaded, and tied down, and setting up the drivers' signals, we were ready to go. We were leaving Dominion Bridge, and as you pull out there, there's a long driveway with cars parked and decorative shrubs all down the right side. Since it was a tricky corner, the drivers had to stay in close touch with each other.

I guess the rear driver never turned his radio on when we did—he turned right but never turned back. As he travelled right, he hit a light pole and three new company cars and caught about a hundred feet of shrubbery. It took us three more hours to get untangled and set things right. We finally got onto the Lougheed Highway, but because of all the messing around we had to park overnight; load restrictions on our permit stated no oversize loads after four p.m. We started off after rush hour the next morning and with a few more delays, we arrived—a day late.

[The moral of this is: Put your ears on and listen!]

Speaking of morals, kind of puts another story into my mind: not exactly an adventure but a small vignette to add to the lunacy that encompasses much of my trucking life.

The Ugly

The truck had been acting strangely: losing power and speed. When I got to Jackass Mountain (just past Boston Bar,B.C.) it quit altogether. Because I had been working on the engine prior to starting this trip, I had a pretty good idea that it was the fuel pump drive. This is about four times the size of a quarter and all you have to do to repair it is take the pump off and replace the drive. It's a half-hour job, if you have the part. The soonest I could get the part from Vancouver was the next day, unless I could get someone to bring it up. The load was going to Kamloops and it was a rush job. After trying to come up with solutions, the only thing I could think of was to ask my wife to bring it up to me. I phoned and after much pleading, she agreed to pick up the part and bring it up.

She didn't like driving by herself at night, so she phoned her girlfriend and her husband, who for the sake of this narrative we will call John and Sally. They were all golf buddies and bridge-playing fiends and they agreed to come up with her. They showed up about three hours later with the part, and Sally and John sat in the car while my wife held the flashlight and helped me put the thing in. After a few minutes I was at the stage where I could finish up by myself, and I told her to go sit in the car and stay warm.

Off she went and to my surprise, she came right back. When I asked her what the problem was, she said that Sally and John were doing the ugly and she would rather wait in the truck with me. She did . . . and I guess they did. But after that, the truck ran fine.

Chapter 7

Dedication to Dougy

This section is dedicated to a good friend who's no longer with us. In later years we were not too close as we lived separate lives; now that he has passed away, I miss him and his goofy humour. The world seems a smaller place without him.

Rest easy, Dougy.

This time I'm rollin' solo, just me and my trusty truck.
We've got to get a goin' so goodbye, and lots of luck!
I'm rollin' up to heaven, up there on the Thunder Road.
They say they're waiting for me and this very special load.
They said to check in with the angel and
the guard shack at heaven's gate.
I guess they need another trucker to
haul some of the holy freight!
So, the next time you see the lightening
and you hear the thunder roar,

Don't you worry about the storm cloud;
It'll be the diesel hummin' as we welcome home one more!

– Author unknown –

In memory of Dougy and his trusty conveyance, known to close friends as Ranjapoor & Clyde! I hope you get a laugh out of his antics.

One time, my son and I were working out of Fort Nelson, B.C., hauling shovel parts to Faro. Because of the weight of the parts, we had to work in the winter, so the ice and snow keep the load from bogging down in the muskeg. On one particular trip, we had a passenger, a good friend and fellow trucker who we'll call Dougy. His truck had broken down and while it was being fixed in Watson Lake, he decided to go to Fort Nelson with us. Because we didn't load until Sunday, we thought when we got to Nelson we would have a couple of drinks. We parked in the Fort Nelson Hotel parking lot and because was minus 35 degrees Fahrenheit, I left the truck running. It was ten a.m. and the bar was open, so we headed inside.

Dougy was a drinker par excellence and had managed to put many guys under the table. On the other hand, my son was not very experienced and I thought I'd better watch that he did not get too drunk. From time to time I tried to phone home from the hotel lobby, but got no answer. I noticed that every time I got back to the bar, I had a full glass of tequila and a beer. After about ten trips out to lobby to try the phone, I was in great shape vocally, and could have shouted that distance. By the time I finally got through on the phone, I couldn't remember why or who I was calling.

Yeah, by this time, I was pretty well lit and my son had already crawled out to the truck. Dougy looked as though he'd just got up, nice and fresh, alert and sober! By 5:30 p.m., it was my turn to head for the truck and a warm bunk. When

I announced I was out of there, Dougy went and sat with a bunch of loggers.

After negotiating the hundred feet from the bar to the truck, I finally made it and crawled up the ladder. When I got inside, Pat was in the bunk passed out, so I sat in the seat and got warmed up. I took my big leather suitcase with the zipper on three sides, opened it up on the doghouse (the divider between the seats in the cab), and just then there was a rap on the window of the truck. When I rolled it down about an inch, I could see a cop standing on the access ladder. He said, "Is there anyone else in the truck?

I said, "Yes" or maybe "Yeah," as the case may be, "my son, why?" He then explained that someone had been on the radio harassing a 15-year-old girl, making obscene remarks and trying to get her to come and join him in the truck. I assured the policeman I would take care of the situation and promised I would not drive anywhere, so he left.

The next thing I knew, I was blind, someone had broken my back and my head was cut off. When I finally realized what had really happened, I would have laughed, except that in my condition that would just about have killed me. I became aware that I had passed out and fallen sideways onto the doghouse. As I did, the suitcase lid closed on my neck and ten hours later, when I woke up, my head was in the suitcase with the zipper of the case lid digging into my neck. My back felt broken and I had the worst hangover I can ever recall. The teeth-marks from the zipper stayed on my neck for three weeks.

I opened a can of veggie soup and was sitting there eating it cold when my son woke up, took one look at me and started to laugh. At this point I said, "Look in the mirror before you laugh at me." I struggled with the gearshift and fumbled my way to our loading area, where I encountered even more laughs. Just then, I saw Dougy, sashaying up the road, whistling and having a great time. When I asked where he'd been, he said when he and his new friends closed the bar, they invited him to a party at their bunkhouse. He woke up, he said, wrapped around a garbage can using a boot for a pillow, but after bacon & eggs and a shot of rum, he was ready to go. Gawd, I hate guys like that . . . especially after he then asked if I wanted him to drive!

On Your Mark

This is another Dougy anecdote to illustrate what a character he was in his younger days.

One day he and I and my son, Pat, unloaded in Faro, Yukon; at least we left our trailers there. The road back to Watson Lake, Yukon, was 247 miles of nothing and bound to be boring. As we were leaving to bobtail back, Dougy said, "Let's see if we can break the time record between here and the lake." I said, "What's the record?" and he said, "Four hours, 45 minutes." Keeping in mind that it was one way, we had five-foot snowbanks and the only traffic was our two trucks and one more that came through on a different day, I thought it was pretty safe. Dougy had a truck that was a little faster than mine; with a top speed of 85 mph compared to my 82 mph.

Since he was quicker, he led off, tearing away to try to set a land (snow) speed record. All went well for about 100 miles, with snow, leaves, birds and rabbits fleeing for dear life. During this ride, my son was holding onto the dash so hard he left fingerprints in it that stayed there for months after. As we were flying along, Dougy, who used to carry a gallon jar of pickles with him at all times, yelled over the CB that he'd had a close call and had nearly gone into the bush. When I asked what had happened he said he'd got his hand caught in the pickle jar while driving. I jokingly asked if he ever got the pickle he was reaching for and he said, "Of course, I had a good one; there's no way I was letting go!"

Shortly after, he called me again and said, "Watch out for the Indians on the road." As I came around the corner, there was a dog sled with six dogs pulling it and an old guy in buckskins hollering at the dogs to go. Sitting in the sled was about 600 pounds of Indian lady. The poor dogs were trying to go straight up the snow-banks on the side of the road and snow was flying as they struggled. I can only imagine there were plenty of curses to accompany the fists shaken at us as we went by. I'm glad the old guy never had a gun or we would have been dead.

When we pulled into Watson Lake, we found we had made it in four hours, 20 minutes: a new record! After we pried my son's hands off the dash, we all went for a drink to celebrate another chapter in the continuing saga of Doug, Dougy and Pat.

> When politicians or truck drivers start talking,
> most people get what's known as Déjà Poo
>
> —the feeling that you've heard all this crap before!

The Trapper

My buddy, Dougy, and I were still hauling shovel parts to Faro from Watson Lake in the Yukon. The road between was a one-lane track for 247 miles of nothing—no garages, gas stations, houses or anything. It was so desolate and forlorn that you had to travel in pairs, in case you had any troubles. Dougy decided one night, in a snowstorm, to sneak out on his own. When he was about 75 miles in, the storm changed into a blizzard. It was really snowing hard and snowstorms can put you to sleep really easily; so in the middle of nowhere, Dougy stopped, got out of his truck and wiped the snow off his lights.

As he finished his back ones, he decided to answer nature's call. There he stood, taking a leak at three a.m. in a raging blizzard out in the middle of nowhere, when this giant hand thumped him on the shoulder and a guy said, "You getting tired, Sonny? How would you like a coffee?" Despite being scared to death and almost having a heart attack, Dougy croaked, "I didn't know anyone lived out here."

"Hell, yes!" the guy answered. "I've lived here for 30 years." Dougy said, "A coffee sounds great! Where's your house?" Then the fellow answered, "It's just 17 miles down there," and he pointed. Dougy looked and through the snow he could make out a dog team sitting at the ready. "I'll bring you back; it's only four hours, round-trip," said the old trapper. Dougy declined, but this is the kind of stuff that happened to him all the time.

Po' Boy

Dougy was the type of guy who, five minutes after he shaved, looked like he hadn't shaved in a week. Besides his ever-present jar of pickles, he always carried with him a loaf of French bread, Kielbasa sausage and a jar of Cheese Whiz. His idea of how to make a good sandwich was split the bread, add everything else and eat! Dougy, in full eating form, combined with the unshaven look, was a scary sight to see. Envision a troll-like creature tearing into this po'boy with the cheese and pickle juice running off his elbows and chin, all over his shirt and anything else that got in the way of the over-spray: he was a hell of a sight!

On one trip, Dougy had a flat at Muncho Lake and we were going to wait for him to get it fixed. I asked him if he was coming for breakfast at the café and he said, "No, I'm going to make a sandwich."

The son of the owner of the motel/café was changing the tire for him. The kid was about 13 years old and while we were having breakfast, he came in and told his dad that he wasn't going to finish the tire because Dougy was scaring him and spraying him with pickle juice and cheese. Apparently, the kid told Dougy that there was a restaurant here and he told the boy that he made the best sandwich in the world. Then he started waving it around and at that point, the kid split. The old man finished fixing the tire, but he told Dougy to stand on the far side of the parking lot until he finished his monster feast.

[One of a Kind!]

Chapter 8

When in a Jam, Spread it on Thick

This chapter chronicles a few close calls or tight spots that I have either been witness to or actually been involved in personally. One of the points I'd like to make in putting these events down on paper is that we often bemoan circumstances that befall us but seldom count our blessings. I guess I'd even have to say that sometimes the blessings come in the form of kids (whether we admit to that or not) and a lot more must surely be put down to someone looking out for us, either by providing a way or giving us the brains to think our own way out of the mess we got ourselves into.

Good Save, Kid

There's a lake on the Alaska Highway called Muncho Lake, where we used to stop for meals or to get a tire fixed. On this particular trip we were running with another truck from Cassiar to Vancouver, and we each had a load of asbestos.

When we pulled in, we parked side by side. My son Pat and I and Ken and his son started to walk toward the restaurant. I noticed that it looked like Ken's truck was moving and then there it was, rolling toward the deep part of the lake.

My son took off on foot, caught up with the truck and climbed in. He managed to stop it about ten feet from the lake. Apparently Ken forgot to apply the brakes when he got out. Lucky thing the kid had fast reflexes. Ken bought the breakfast that morning.

Snowed

Another close call I experienced was when I was taking a load of pipe to a new dam, 90 miles north of Revelstoke B.C. By the time I got to Hope it had started to snow very heavily. I had trouble seeing the road as I started down the hill toward the lake by Three Valley Gap. At the bottom of the hill, the road turns left and continues along the lake. On the right, there is a small motel, about ten feet below the level of the road. I had just started down the hill when a huge gust of wind came up the lake, carrying enough snow that I couldn't see a thing. It was an enormous whiteout, and because of ice and snow on the road, I was in a dilemma. I couldn't stop completely, because if I applied the brakes too fast, I would start to slide. I couldn't see a foot in front of me and I had no idea where either edge of the road was. The only thing I could remember was that on the motel side, there was a small curb for runoff for rain and a driveway for the motel. On the other side, the road sloped toward the lake. I was driving from memory and sense of touch!

I went around that corner at about 25 mph, hoping I was turning in the right spot; then continued to creep along until the whiteout started to lift. It had extended about 100 feet past the corner. Finally, I could see the road. When at last I stopped, I sat on the edge of the road and shook for about ten minutes before I was calm enough to continue. It was a pretty scary thing—one I did not want to go through again.

Smelly

One predicament occurred when my son and I were hauling chlorine tanks from Tacoma, Washington to Mackenzie. The tanks are eight feet long by two and a half feet and to load them they were placed crosswise and then chained from the front of the trailer to the rear. After we got the gas unloaded, the taps were tightened so they wouldn't leak any left-over gas and we headed back with the empties. By the time we got back to Williams Lake and started down into town, we decided we would stop at an A & W that was halfway down the hill.

When I pulled over, the shoulder gave way and the truck and trailer had a real good lean on it. Now it looked as though a load of chlorine was headed for the A & W. Several people stopped and saw the small danger stickers. About this time a small tow truck stopped and asked if we needed any help. Just as the tow truck was getting ready to hook on to try to move the truck, the RCMP arrived. When the cop looked at the situation and saw the stickers on the tanks, he cleared everybody out of the area and radioed for a big tow truck. It became a little more urgent when he smelled chlorine— (the valves do not seal very well). Because everything was going well, I never told anyone that the tanks were empty. As a matter of fact, I found some more danger stickers and put some of them on the tanks to get everyone working like crazy.

The big tow truck hooked on the truck and pulled it right out of its precarious position. As soon as we were out, the cop said, "Get that thing out of here. No charge for the tow truck since it was a biological situation." Phew!

Hoser

Mechanical problems crop up everywhere when you're driving big machines. This occurrence took place when I had a load of miscellaneous goods bound for a gold mine up near Cassiar. As I turned off near Kitwanga, which is close to Hazelton, B.C., I heard a strange noise coming from the truck. The noise grew louder and louder as I proceeded and by the time I had gone a few miles, I knew I had to stop and see if I could find the cause. When I exited the truck, I could smell something hot and I followed my nose till I located it. I could see that the front wheel bearing was red hot. I jacked the axle up and the wheel could not turn—the bearing was seized up. After I pulled the wheel off, the hub wouldn't turn; it was so hot that all the grease had burned up and the whole thing was glowing red. The only way I could touch it was with my gloves on. I couldn't do much without the proper tools!

When it was finally cool enough to work on I took the hammer and chisel and beat the crap out of it until I was able to remove the hub and the outer race of the bearing. The inner half of the bearing was welded to the spindle (the part of the wheel that mounts to the axle and steers the truck). All I had to work with were a hammer, a chisel and a hacksaw. Because the bearing race is made of extra-hard steel, I could barely put a mark on it; what I needed was a cutting torch.

On the front of the trailer of stuff destined for the mine were about 20 tanks or bottles of oxygen and 12 tanks of acetylene, exactly what you need to fuel a torch. With these and hoses and regulators, it could be a complete cutting torch. I searched the Bill of Lading and the load; but it was no dice on the remaining necessities.

As I sat there, contemplating about a thousand-dollar tow bill back to Prince George (which I figured was the closest place to get it fixed), a logging truck pulled up and the driver asked what the problem was. He said he had a torch and hoses etc. in his shop that I could borrow and he also had a bearing I could buy. Very thankfully, I took him up on his offer and he left and was back in about ten minutes; his shop was only a mile up the road. What a break!

He had the right bearing and he was so helpful. It took about three hours to get the race off with the torch, because I had to be careful to get all the fused (welded) junk off without damaging the spindle—if I did, I was screwed big time. It continued to be my lucky day! After using a borrowed file, I managed to clean it up enough that everything fit. When I had it back together, I took the hose and other stuff back and told the guy he saved my life. You might say I thanked him pro*hose*ly. My back haul from the mine that trip was a four by four box full of gold . . . but that's another story.

Strive for progress, not perfection.

Chapter 9

Not-So-Easy Fixes

Still on the subject of predicaments, while hauling a load of pipe for a drill rig, my son and I were about a hundred miles into the Northwest Territories when we came to one-lane bridge with metal sides about 8 ½ feet wide. The problem was the ramp onto the bridge was at a 45-degree angle and the only part we could get onto the bridge was the tractor; there was no way that the trailer would go on at that angle. Due to the elevation of the ramp we figured the only solution was to jack the trailer up and put some sheets of greased plywood under the tires, so they would slide sideways. After we had it set up, I went ahead until the trailer was lined up against the bridge rail and pulled. As I pulled, the wheels on the greased plywood slid around until they straightened out and lined up with the bridge. While I was pulling, the metal on both the trailer and the bridge was grinding and screeching and I was hoping the rails would stay on the bridge; if not, we would be in the river.

Once across, I got out having a look at the situation. All the rope hooks on the trailer were gone and the bridge rails were scraped up, but we were safely over the bridge. On the way back, it was a lot easier as there was no load and the rig slid a lot better around the corner.

Leaf springs on a truck are part of the suspension system which keeps a vehicle suspended off the ground and eases the amount of bounce to give a smoother ride. In heavy vehicles, like semis, the spring is made up of several arc-shaped pieces of spring steel, known as leaves, stacked on top of each other, and it rides under the axle. In the middle of one trip in northern B.C. a front spring broke (every leaf except the main one). Since we were 300 miles from the nearest town, Watson Lake, and I hadn't yet reached my drop-off destination, I had to try and think of something that would allow me to get there that did not entail a tow truck or a long wait for the parts.

I found a piece of oak blocking on my load and, using a flattened-out five-gallon oil can, I wrapped the wood with the tin and nailed it together. I managed to locate a bunch of pieces of inner tube and nailed those to the tin. Then I jacked the spring back in place. When I had enough room, I put the wood-tin replacement spring in place of the broken one and chained it in place. Then I let the weight down and away I went. It was a pretty rough ride but I went another hundred miles, unloaded and headed back to Watson Lake, where I picked up a load for Los Angles. After dodging all the scale checks, I got the spring fixed in L.A. The spring shop said I had done a great job of patching it up.

What A Bag!

On the newer tractors, all the rear suspension is done with air bags and in the north-country, everyone carries one or two spare bags. Two bags is usually enough, for sure. On one particular trip, I blew a second bag and I had already used up my spares. I had no others to replace it. The trailer dropped down onto the tires and it couldn't go anywhere. From what I had been told, I was screwed. There was no way to adjust it so it would be usable.

Being that I am a person who never gives up—especially if I've been told it can't be done—I took my tools and a bunch of nails and rivets and crawled under the truck, to start plugging air lines using nails for the plugs. If I needed about half the air, I plugged up the airline by using nails with half the head cut off. By closing off some lines and leaving some wide open, I put extra air into the one next to the blown bag; and by adjusting the control arms, I managed to get about four inches of space. Although it took five hours to do all the changes, by taking it easy, I was able to run on the makeshift airbag system and to deliver the load. I even managed to pick up another load, and by carefully loading it on the correct side, I delivered the full backhaul of lumber to Vancouver. When I took the truck in to get it fixed, the mechanic took a look and said it was an impossibility to run on three bags, and because I had changed all the control arms, he said he could not adjust it. He had to replace all the arms and valves. I reckon the impossible takes a little additional thought!

Too Hot to Handle

On a trip to Whitehorse, we got fuel at a truck stop in the Yukon, and after an hour's driving, an injector seized up. The knocking kept getting worse so I got out my bar (a two and a half foot long metal piece used to tighten belts or cables on the load) and used it as a stethoscope to detect which injector was failing. I had to remove the push rod, because if I didn't it would soon go through the block of the engine. To remove the rocker cover in minus 40-degree temperature called for some ingenuity. The engine was red hot and if it was shut off for even five minutes, it probably would not restart. I began by jacking up the cab and removing the rocker cover while trying to blot up the red-hot oil (keeping in mind that the engine was still running and everything was hot). When I had all the bolts loosened and the injector was ready to come out, I shut the engine off, and with burning fingers, removed the injector and after that, the push rod. Once the injector was out I could see rust on it, which told me the Yukon fuel we pumped in must have had water in it. I discarded the rod and reinstalled the injector. Fortunately, the truck started right away and I carried on toward Vancouver with five cylinders operating. About 50 miles later, I had the go through the whole thing again as a second one went. I was lucky the truck could actually run on four cylinders: not much power, but we made it!

Lost and Found

One winter, we were hauling shovel parts from Fort Nelson to Whitehorse. We were only allowed to do this delivery in winter, because the loads were so heavy, they had to be hauled on frozen roads only. We were using a low-bed trailer, which is about four feet lower in the centre than a normal trailer and stronger. It is made for hauling heavy machinery. After we got the shovel tracks loaded and chained down, we took off in a convoy of four trucks. I was third in the row; it was snowing hard and impossible to see your trailer behind you or your load. We were pretty much plowing snow, and, as we went by this frozen lake and were climbing a hill alongside it, the guy behind me called my CB, saying, "Hey, Doug, you just lost something."

I checked the mirrors and couldn't see a thing, so I stopped and got out and walked back to his truck. "What did I lose?" I asked. He said, "It looked like a couple of tires." When I asked where they went, he said the last time he saw them, they were headed down the bank taking 40-foot bounces about a half-mile down the lake. From the big dents in the snow, where they had bounced, we could see the trail heading for and traveling across the icy surface of the lake. We went and looked at the trailer and sure enough, the two rear wheels on the trailer were gone. The bearing had broken and wheels, tires and all had bounded up the lake. Because the bearing was gone, the axle wasn't usable, so I got out my biggest chain, jacked up the axle and chained it to the frame of the trailer. By the time I was finished, all I had to do was plug the airline to keep the brakes working on the rest of the truck and trailer. We made it to Whitehorse with no more trouble. Doctor Doug had done it again!

Chapter 10

Dust and Blusters

My son and I had a load on headed for Snag, Yukon. It was a TV satellite dish and this was my very first trip to Snag, a village on a dry-weather side road off the Alaska Highway. It's just north of Beaver Creek, Yukon. As you can imagine, there wasn't a lot of pavement or even any decent roads, let alone freeway. In fact, there was about four inches of dust on the track we were travelling and there wasn't anything that wasn't full of dust. Dust was on the road, in the cab of the truck and all over our suitcases, in our hair and it felt like we were eating it, too. It was so thick that on the roadway, it looked like brown water with waves coming off the wheels of the truck.

In this area, there are no large trees other than poplar; these are about six or eight inches 'round and about 20 feet high and this side road cuts through the sparse stands. As we travelled along, you could hardly see a thing because any dust that had been raised by anyone or anything hung in the air like fog and took forever to settle. I thought I heard a crashing noise and then the sound of things breaking, so I stopped the truck to check it out. The noise got louder and louder and was coming from the road ahead. All I could see through the dust was the tops of the trees moving around and then, as we watched, a giant oil rig pulled by a massive truck loomed out of the dust. The cracking noise was being made by this twenty-five-foot-wide pile of rusty old angle iron and steel plate that was almost 45 feet high. The breaking noise was the snapping of all the trees on both sides of the road as this huge truckload barrelled along. The rig took up the entire road—and then some.

We spoke to the guys moving the rig, and we came to the decision that there was only one way we were going to go any-where and that was if we drove under the edge of the platform on the oil rig carrier. To get under meant we had to take off our exhaust pipes to get the height down from over 13 feet to under 12 feet, 6 inches. We got the oil-rig guys to move over as far as they could and we crawled along under the edge of the deck and back onto the road. I really wanted to get a picture of that manoeuver but my Polaroid was out of commission—plugged with dust! After we got the truck put back together again, we took off for Snag. The rest of the way it was easy to make out the edge of the road through the dust: no trees!

Don't Turn Off, Eh?

Here's another tale of someone who thought he knew a lot about trucking and didn't listen to advice. He was convinced he knew more than I (or anyone else) did. It all started when a guy I knew in Los Angeles phoned and asked if he could go on a trip with us. I told him he could, if he could find his own way to our place in Surrey. When I arrived home with a load of steel going to Revelstoke, he was waiting at the house. I told him that if he was going to sleep on the trip, it would have to be in the seat. I also said that if Pat or I were awake when he was, he would have to either sit on the doghouse (padded area between the seats) or ride in the sleeper, if weren't in it.

Basically, he was told to stay out of the way. He agreed and we set out for Revelstoke. We arrived there with no problems, except the temperature was minus 30 degrees and it was plenty cold. From Revelstoke, we had to travel 90 miles to a new dam that B.C. Hydro was building north of town. When I was unloaded, I phoned for a back haul and they sent us to Radium Hot Springs, which is south toward Cranbrook. When we arrived, it was too late to load, so the shipper booked us a double room at a hotel. I told my buddy that we could get another room, or Pat could stay in the truck, as it had to be kept running. If we shut it off, it would be hard to start in the morning. He insisted he would stay in the truck. I agreed and told him where the heaters and electric blankets were. I also set the idle and reiterated the instructions about not shutting the engine off.

Pat and I took off. We had dinner and then we hit the sack. The shipper picked us up at six in the morning and at that time it was minus 35 degrees. When we got to the truck, it was not running and when I climbed in, the dummy was in the bunk, wrapped up in all the blankets. I asked why the truck was shut off and he said he got too hot, so he turned it off.

I asked him, "Do you remember the last thing I said to you was not to turn the engine off?"

He said, "Yes." By this time I let out a bunch of expletives slandering his mother, his ancestry, his sexual preferences and his lack of intelligence. He then told me that it was only off for four hours; and this started me off, again. I told him that at minus 35 degrees the batteries are so cold that a half-hour or maybe even five minutes would be too long.

When I tried to start the truck, it wouldn't even make a sound. We had to take the batteries to the shipper's place and sit them on the furnace vents in his office. The oil was so cold in the engine, it was almost solid, and I had to build a fire under the oil pan to get it warmed up. We got the batteries back in by about three p.m. and with jumper cables from the guy's pick-up and some ether starting fluid, finally got it going. By this time is was too late to get loaded, so we stayed in the truck and the wise guy spent a cold, uncomfortable night in the front seat.

Over this whole thing, I lost one day and by the time we got to town it was Saturday and I could not get unloaded. I ended up having to pay $50 to get a preload and $75 to get my back haul unloaded—all thanks to a know-it-all bloody idiot!

Chapter 11

Cover Your Ass

Human nature being what it is, business people in all walks of life have to keep a keen eye on those they deal with lest they get taken to the cleaners or robbed blind by unscrupulous parties. This chapter contains a few stories of times when I felt it was prudent to cover my ass, as it were!

I've been lucky enough to see some gorgeous scenery in my travels, particularly along the west coast of Canada and the U.S. My load on this particular day was ten lifts of spruce plywood, and normally the backhaul would be ten lifts of fir plywood out of the same mill we delivered to in Roseburg, Oregon. This time, I was to go to Yreka, California and haul back a load of redwood. To get there, I had to go to Grants Pass, Oregon and head for Crescent City, California.

It was quite a trip, going over to the coast. A good portion of it was through Redwood National Park. When you're weaving through those fantastic woods, you really feel insignificant.

Some of the trees are enormous and the road winds in amongst them. It's truly beautiful driving through that area.

When we reached Crescent City, we turned right and headed for the mill. At the mill, I found that we were to haul eight lifts of redwood to Vancouver, B.C. Getting ready to load, I saw that the dunnage (blocking, usually waste material, to go under the load) was all four-by-three redwood pieces, four feet long. I asked the shipper if I could take any extra pieces and he said, "Help yourself, take all you want." At the time, I was building a bar in the basement of my home and this wood would be perfect, so I loaded about 50 pieces under the load. I thanked the guy and before we took off, I had the shipper sign a paper for me saying that he had given them to me (to prove I hadn't stolen them). He was happy to and said he hoped my bar turned out well. I gave him my phone number and told him if he was ever in Canada, to give me a call and I would serve him a drink from the bar. He said he'd do that. He never called, so I guess he never made it; nevertheless, I've had a few drinks in his honour.

When I arrived at the company in Burnaby and started to unload, I piled the blocks on the back of the truck.

 The receiver came out and said they belonged to him since it was his load. I said, "Sorry, to disappoint you, but this Bill of Lading says they are a gift to me." I offered him two pieces from under each lift. He was fairly upset and phoned the company I worked for, but when they learned of the Bill of Lading, they told him that they were mine. Those Redwood pieces made a hellofa bar!

A Weighty Problem

In a completely different scenario, once, after taking a load to Terrace, my back haul was from Kitimat. It consisted of a large metal roller that was covered with rubber. These rollers come in different sizes and they're used in the pulp mills for rolling wood chips into paper. Periodically, they have to be sent to Vancouver to be re-covered with rubber.

When I backed into the shed to get loaded, I asked the shipper, because of the various sizes and weights, how much did the one I was carrying weigh? His reply was 30,000 pounds, which was fine since we could haul 40,000 pounds or a bit more, if it was loaded properly.

I was standing by the trailer as he loaded it and as it landed on the deck, the trailer creaked and groaned and the tires looked half flat; it was pretty obvious that the roller was a lot more than 30,000 pounds. When I commented on this he said, "No way could it weigh more, that's the weight on the Bill of Lading." Since I was responsible for any overload tickets, I told the shipper that I wished to speak to his boss and wanted verification of the weight in writing.

After about an hour of arguing with the boss, and letting him know that without written verification, I wouldn't take the load, he made out a new Bill of Lading and gave me a piece of paper that verified the exact weight of 30,000 pounds, saying that if there was any discrepancy it was entirely their responsibility, so I agreed to take it.

I tarped up the load and chained it down, then I took off. As you leave Kitimat, there is a slight hill out of town; just pulling up that hill, the truck was really working hard. When I drove onto the scales in Terrace, the scale guy flashed the sign that said, "Bring papers." When I went inside, he started laughing so hard he could hardly talk. "Okay," I said, "How much over?" He answered that as near as he could figure my gross weight was about 25,000 pounds overweight and by his figuring, instead of weighing 30,000 pounds, the roller weighed 30 tons or 60,000 pounds.

I showed him my registration, Bill of Lading, and the nice letter from the Superintendent, swearing to the 30,000-pound weight. I had phoned Arrow from Kitimat and explained the whole thing; now I phoned them from the scales and they said, "Get all the permits and the copies of the tickets you're issued and e-mail them to the Superintendent; then continue on slowly." The fine was $900 and the permit was $1,200. After I collected my papers and was getting in the truck, the inspector said, "That was a smart thing you did and you saved yourself a bunch of money."

I said, "I'm glad I had enough sense to cover my butt."

That roller was so heavy that I could feel every bump; it was like being out on the ocean. I finally arrived at Lac La Hache, where the trailer broke in half; so I sat there for three days while a machine shop from Cache Creek fixed it. That was an expensive trip for that Superintendent; the fines, the permits, three days' wages and three days' repair costs. I was sure glad that I'd remember to live by the warning: Cover Your Ass.

Chapter 12

No Mud in the House

Mud

One day in April during break-up (for the uninitiated, that's when the frost comes out of the ground and things in the north become very muddy and the roads become impassable), we were heading to Whitehorse. Shortly after I turned off the main highway and headed for Meziadin Junction, the road deteriorated badly, with more mud and holes to push your way through than there was road. I was just approaching a very large puddle of mud and water when I noticed something a little out of place. There was a D8 Cat parked right there but not a soul around. I couldn't figure that out—not until I started into the hole. The mud was so deep, it came into the cab and I was sure glad I had a cab-over tractor! Within moments, there was about three inches of mud in the cab and I finally realized what the cat was there for: pulling you out! I should have fastened a chain on first, but now the bumper was under about three feet of mud. After fishing around to locate the bumper with no success, I finally got out, fired up the Cat and went to the back of the trailer. I got the Cat lined up and pushed until the bumper and the tractor were out. Then I put a chain on and pulled the rig the rest of the way out. When the truck was finally out of the puddle, everything was covered in mud. Luckily, it was a diesel and the air cleaner was elevated; if it had been a gas engine, it would have been toast. I was thankful that some thoughtful soul had left the Cat there. When I arrived in Meziadin, it took me two hours to get the mud off of and out of everything.

As you leave the junction, you need to turn right if you're headed for Whitehorse, and as I was getting ready to pull out, a driver coming south radioed that the hill out of the junction was pretty slippery. I told him about the hole he was headed for and warned him to put the chain on first. We went our separate ways and as I turned right and started up the hill, I realized it was really muddy. I only managed to get about a hundred yards before I spun out and had to climb out to hang my chains in a foot of mud. I was *not* a happy trucker, as anyone within five miles could probably tell. I finally made it up the hill and went to take my chains off; they were coated with mud and so was the truck! Eventually I reached Whitehorse and had another turn at cleaning off the mud. Being a rational person, as most truckers are, I went home by a different route: the Alaska Highway. It took a lot longer but it was much cleaner!

Our aim in life improves as we grow older,
but by then we've mostly run out of ammunition.

House

Another odd situation my son and I ran into was when we were to haul a load that consisted of a complete prefab house. The haul was for a business from New Westminster. We would have the whole house on, including windows, doors, shingles and nails; all in all, everything that was needed to build a two-bedroom house.

We were told it would be ready for pick-up on Sunday afternoon and it had to be in Kamloops Monday morning. On Sunday, when we drove into the prefab company's back lot, I noticed that the front end of the trailer was sitting on an angle and was quite low to the ground. It appeared as though, when the crew loaded it, they didn't notice that one landing gear (the part that holds the front of the trailer up until the tractor is hooked up) had been set down on a deteriorated section of pavement. It was basically soft dirt and I guess after it sat for a couple of days it sank eight or ten inches into the ground. I backed up to it and the fifth wheel wouldn't fit under it.

There was no one around to help, since it was the weekend. We took out the jack and found a bunch of blocks to try to raise it, with no luck; it just kept sliding off. As we travelled back and forth with the tractor trying to get hooked up, the pin on the trailer slipped over the frame rail on the tractor— we were really stuck now! We couldn't go ahead or back up. Finally I tried to phone a tow truck: no service, what next!?

We spotted a couple of forklifts went down to investigate, but everything was locked up. As we were snooping around the watchman came to the gate and asked what we were doing. We explained our problem and he said, "Sorry, there's nothing I can do."

I said, "For $50 could you unlock the gate and disappear for fifteen minutes?"

He said "$60 and you've got a deal." We climbed on the fork-lifts and headed to the truck. We put one lift truck on each side and the load came right up. When it was high enough, we blocked it up, moved the tractor under it and hooked up. We had the lift trucks back in less than 15 minutes and there were a couple of happy drivers and a happy watchman. We made it to Kamloops on time.

Sometimes, you have to be a little inventive.

Chapter 13

BRR Below Zero

Ice Icicles

Travelling in the north country, northern B.C., Yukon, Northwest Territories and Alaska, can be a great blessing and a great trial. Not only is this country a never-ending source of headaches, large and small, with endless clouds of dust, endless clouds of bugs, and endless crowds of tourists, but it also comprises endless miles of the most beautiful country you can imagine. The dust lies on the side roads five or six inches deep when it's not in the air or in your eyes, ears and any other orifices you would care to mention. The bugs are so big, it's been said that three mosquitoes can haul away a full-grown man and you need wiper blades on your glasses to keep some bit of visibility. Not only do 'skeeters end up in the same spots as the dust, when you must answer the call of nature, you have to be extra careful about where else they might end up.

While it could be said that the tourists fit into the same category as the dust and the bugs, because they definitely turn out in swarms, many come unprepared for the heat of the summer or the cold that characterizes fall and winter in the far north. (Believe it or not, in the summer, it can be really hot.) Just like truckers, visitors should be sure to carry water, food, car parts, fan belts, wrenches, maps, bug spray and bear spray, spare tires (the gravel roads eat them), satellite phones, flares, mosquito netting, more bug spray—and hopefully the bear spray holds out. Those who overstay the warm part of the year have it good in some respects but have an added list of precautions to take.

The endless clouds of bugs depart with the bulk of the tourists and the dust is transformed into white stuff that sticks to roads, cars and also to wolves and bears until they show how smart they are by going to bed for several months. You still need to carry fan belts, spares, satellite phones, food, water, wrenches and flares—but now you must also remember antifreeze, canned heat, warmer clothes, boots, gas, snowshoes, snowmobiles, a decent supply of rye, and anything else you can think of to keep warm. The bar in the Whitehorse Hotel is a good spot to plan your warm excursions, when you know the weather can get cold enough to freeze your reproductive parts off.

While I was driving in the winter, hauling to Whitehorse and Faro or wherever it seemed coldest, my truck was equipped with heaters under the seats, one on the dash, and one in the sleeper; a huge heating pad under the mattress and an electric blanket. That assortment of heat producers would keep it really warm (like T-shirt warm) and the set-up was extremely nice: after loading in arctic weather, just crawl in and warm up in no time.

The only problem was, when it was minus 50 degrees or colder, you would wake up in the morning and the condensation from your breath would be frozen on the ceiling of the sleeper, forming icicles eight to ten inches long. It did tend to make you put on more clothes or crawl back under the electric blanket. Still, nothing I can imagine can beat the north country for its endless miles of beautiful scenery, in any season.

Minus Sixty-two Degrees

On one memorable trip I was taking a load of pipe to an oil rig in the Northwest Territories. When we loaded in Richmond, it was snowing very hard, so it was difficult loading. There was snow between the layers of pipe and it was really hard to tie the load down. We got it done, eventually, and headed for the freeway. I don't remember too many other trips that started in the snow and went north into more snow.

We progressed up the Fraser Canyon and by the time we reached Cache Creek, we had needed to tighten the load down four times; the snow had not let up. At the junction, we turned toward Williams Lake, Quesnel and Prince George. From there we went up toward the Alaska Highway, by way of Fort St. John, where we fuelled up, as there were not a lot of truck stops from the Fort to our destination. By this time, the temperature was minus 25 degrees and the forecast said it was going down to minus 35 degrees. The heaters, rad cover, front cover and belly tarp under the cab were working overtime. In a cab-over tractor, all there is for warmth is a sheet of aluminium, a cab cover and a rad cover. One good thing is that the snow had quit, at least for the time being.

By the time we reached Fort Nelson, it was down to minus 30 degrees. Our instruction said to turn right on a logging road and our destination was 175 miles north. We stocked up on fuel, food, water, and de-icers for fuel, door locks, wipers, windshields and mirrors. The mirrors and windshield were heated and even so, they froze up as we went farther north. Travelling up that logging road, there were fewer and fewer tire tracks. We kept struggling along and in one place there was a river about 40 feet wide, and it was frozen solid. The only bridge had a "Closed" sign on it and there was a second sign that read "Cross Here" with a large arrow pointed at the river bank on the right side of the bridge.

So there we were, crossing a frozen (hopefully) river, 100 miles from nowhere. If the ice was too thin, we would be in a bad spot. It was so cold that it seemed unlikely that the ice wouldn't be thick enough—after all, they put up a sign that said where to cross. But what did they use as a criterion on ice safety: a 2,000-pound pick-up or an 84,000-pound 18-wheeler?

Our first job was to chain up. If the ice started to crack, the chains might possibly help. As we set out, I had my son Pat walking ahead of the truck to see if there was any obvious movement or change in the contour of the ice. Just as he walked out onto the ice, his feet went out from under him and he slid about 60 feet downriver and disappeared around a corner. As soon as I lost my spotter, I just went ahead and didn't pay any attention to all the creaking, groaning and cracking of the ice; and I made it across with no trouble at all.

As I was taking my chains off, Pat came walking back. He said he'd slid around the corner for about 20 feet before he finally got his footing and walked back. He also said he was damned cold because he'd lost his mitts. After a quick look, he found them—a good thing because it was getting colder and now the wind was starting to blow. The temperature on the truck thermometer was now at minus 30 degrees. Our next landmark was an airport with a drilling rig on the edge of it. After about 25 miles, it had really started to blow and we stumbled onto the one runway of dirt and rocks. It was blowing so hard that most of the snow had blown away. We bundled up with everything we had, including a scarf over the mouth to keep our lungs from freezing and fur-lined mitts with fur-lined glove liners. I had parked with the cab away from the wind, all the heaters going full blast and the rpms of truck really high, trying to get some heat. By this time, the guys working there said it was minus 37 degrees and with 40-mph winds, the wind chill, as near as they could figure out was minus 62. When we got out to untie the load, the belts were frozen solid and we had to beat them with hammers to get them to bend, so we could get them off. You could only spend about five minutes at the job and then you had to get back in the truck. The first time I got back in, my scarf was frozen to my beard, my glasses were frozen to my face and any exposed skin was a deep purple. Besides that, I had frostbite on one finger, right through the two pairs of fur-line gloves.

When we finally got the belts off, they were so stiff they couldn't be rolled up so we had to put them on the trailer in a heap and tie them down with rope from inside the truck. Through all this, I was worried that it would get colder. I knew if it did, we would be in big trouble because Diesel fuel turns to jelly at about minus 70 degrees Fahrenheit and that would have been game over! If the truck shut off at low temperatures, unless you had heated fuel tanks and heated batteries, you were screwed!

After they got us unloaded, we set off slowly for warmer temperatures. With no load, the river was a piece of cake! As we crossed the ice, it started to snow and it continued to snow all the way home; even when we got to Vancouver, it was still snowing, but it was warm enough to finally roll our belts up. This trip had been my coldest experience, ever, and I have no desire to try and break my record. Minus 62 degrees is as cold as I ever want to be!

Frozen Nuts

A further cold weather experience I had was on another trip to Whitehorse. When I left Vancouver it was in the middle of an odd cold spell; the temperature was minus ten and the further north you went, the colder it became. At Prince George, 500 miles from Vancouver, it was minus 25 degrees. By the time I had driven to Hazelton, it was minus 40. I turned off there and headed for Meziadin Junction, where the road turned to either Stewart or Whitehorse.

As I was approaching the junction, I could hear some strange noises coming from the front end of the truck. When I checked it out, I discovered that four wheel nuts on the left front wheel had broken off. When I looked at the other side, five had gone. I got on the CB to Stewart, where Arrow had a shop, and they told me I probably had metal fatigue in the studs, a condition accelerated by the extreme cold. When I asked what the temperature was in Stewart and he said that it was minus 52 degrees! Brrrrr

Frozen Balls and Misdirections

Over the years, I travelled to some weird and wonderful places and was involved in some strange escapades. One such trip was a load of grinding balls (for smashing ore). These were to go to a small mine at Fort St. James. Never having been there, I had to ask directions of one of the locals at the Fort. He said to cross the tracks and turn left, then drive alongside the tracks for 18 miles and we would come right to the mine.

As we drove alongside the tracks, we saw absolutely nothing. At about mile 14, we met an empty dump truck and, on the narrow road, he was just able to squeeze by. He stopped along beside my truck and we said "Hi" to one another and he asked where I was going. When I told him, he laughed and said, "Not on this road; you should have turned right at the crossroad and it takes you right to the mine." I asked where the first place was that I could turn around. He laughed again and told me there wasn't one! The biggest spot on the road would just accommodate his dump truck.

I said, "Are you positive?" and he said, "Absolutely! There is barely room for my truck."

At this point I began to think of my options, which took about one second, since there was only one option and that was to back up for 14 miles, which I then set out to do. The only thing that kept me going was planning my revenge on the guy who gave me those bogus directions. It took three hours and the help of a great many swear words and much fuming to get back to the crossing. Once there, I turned around and found the right road, so I finally managed to get to the mill and get unloaded. Very frustrating!

Chapter 14

Snowing Off and On

Show-Off

My son, Pat, has been bugging me to include a certain story about a trip to Penticton with an empty trailer down the Hope-Princeton Highway. It took some pretty strong persuasion, but here it is: On this particular day, we had our load delivered and were heading home; all was going well. With a new truck that sported all the bells and whistles: 450 hp Cummins Diesel, an Allison seven-speed automatic transmission, nice new Arrow paint job . . . I guess I was kind of showing off the new wheels.

Just at The Falls, it started to snow and by the time we actually got to The Falls hill, there was about two inches of packed, wet snow. As I rounded the first corner, the truck, with all the new tires, power divider and the super-superior skills of the driver (me), managed to get stuck sideways on the hill.

I spent about an hour trying to get straight and back down. I finally had to quit and wait for a sand truck and while I sat there, I had to listen to about 200 trucks and cars talking on the CB about some idiot that spun out on the little hill.

When the sand truck arrived and I got mobile once again, I had to run the gauntlet of all those vehicles held up because of my predicament and I had to listen to all the disparaging remarks. Now you can see why I didn't relish the idea of putting this episode down on paper.

Freak snowfall or the price of vanity?

Trapper Talk

Pat and I had a load out of Vancouver to a drill site in the Northwest Territories. The directions were in the language of a trapper on his trap line. As an example: 27 miles past Lone Trapper Trail, turn . . . as if you could see any signs that told you anything! The first sign we did see was for Cabin Creek Road, which was the turn-off from the Alaska Highway. As we took the turn-off, we wondered what we were getting into. The snow on the side of the road was really deep; the roads were all plowed—but they were plowed out one way. We were trying to follow the instructions and they said, "After 45 miles, take the left turn and proceed to mile 26 on Broken Bow Road." The only problem was the signposts were four feet high and the snow was five feet deep! Anyway, whoever came up with the directions never took that into consideration. At each corner we passed, we could see the road sign: a piece of stick poking out of the snow. Finally, after becoming hopelessly lost, we met a house-mover pulling an office trailer, part of an oil rig.

There was barely enough room but he squeezed in beside our window and asked, "Where are you going?" When I told him the rig site number he could barely suppress his laughter. "You should have turned off about 28 miles back and then gone 15 miles to the airport." When I asked how he read the signs, he said he didn't because he had made the trip about 25 times now, and he remembered the road.

I said, "How do I find the turn-off?" and he said, "Don't worry about that; I've got a can of red paint, I'll paint the corner red, but that's not your main problem."

I said, "Yeah? What is?" and he told me there was no place to turn around.

I asked him, "What about where you picked up the trailer?"

He said, "No chance! The trailer was facing the right way, so there wasn't any turning around needed. There's no turn-around and no roads other than the one you missed 28 miles back."

Pat and I had no choice but to continue on and hope we could find a way. Finally, we found a fork in the road with a side road facing the other way, so I got over to the edge and went back and forth flattening the snow on the edge of the road. It became a game after that, flatten the snow, go ahead, back up, go ahead, back up a foot, go ahead two feet. By the time we had done the impossible and got turned around, 5 ½ hours had passed, but we were headed the right way. We finally arrived at the airport. Someone was starting to complain that we were two hours late and it was the first I had heard of the time limit—too bad! I was *not* going to take any crap because of wrong directions and mixed-up signs.

That was the worst damn U-turn, *ever*!

What a Reception!

This story took place on a trip to Whitehorse. There were six trucks involved and we were hauling beer and various cases of alcohol. Sometimes, it gets really boring and hard to stay awake on the road, especially in the middle of the night. Just before dawn is the worst. When we were in the middle of the back end of nowhere, we would tell dirty jokes over the radio and when we ran out of those, we'd switch to limericks. As the night progressed we would start to invent or make up our own, some of which were pretty gross.

As we talked, we decided that whoever had the most creative limerick would win breakfast, paid for by the other five drivers. The judges were to be the four passengers riding in the different trucks. Mile after mile, we stayed alert and tried to top each other with originality and smut. Just after someone came up with a truly rank entry and we were carrying on a conversation amongst us about it, a female voice piped up and said, "That was the best one, yet!"

There was dead silence for a minute and then someone said, in a very feminine voice, "I live on a ranch about 100 miles from White Horse. Our place is in the back country with no neighbours. The only entertainment we have is the CB radio. I don't sleep much, so I eavesdrop. Normally, I don't say anything, but I enjoyed this battle so much, I had to speak out and tell you that I think the winner is number four." She'd picked our winner. She told us her handle was Yukon Sal and asked us to give her a call when we went passing through. I didn't win the contest, but over the years I had many conversations with her, and they kept me awake for many miles. Thanks, Sal, from the Fugitive.

One-third of a Truck

On a cold windy day, I stopped in at our dispatch in North Vancouver and received a load of lumber from New Westminster to Portland, Oregon. My backhaul was from Tucson, Arizona to Sparwood, B.C. with a further backhaul from Revelstoke to Vancouver. It was to be quite a long, winding trip.

After whooping it up because we were going to a warm place, two trucks went to New Westminster to load, with four more trucks to follow. The six of us were to bring back as much of a huge earthmoving truck as we could. After we were loaded, we headed out. The trip to Portland went smoothly and after fueling up there, we headed southeast to central Oregon, where we turned south and proceeded through Oregon and Nevada. It was a long, tiring trip and by the time we got to Tucson in Arizona, we were pretty beat.

By this time, there were only two of us, Fred and myself; the other guys got lost looking for shortcuts. When we had a look at the machine sitting in Caterpillar's yard, it was in pieces, since it was too huge to haul any other way. My piece turned out to be one-third of the dump-box. Even cut into thirds, it was almost too big for one load and it was really hard to tie down. (It was so oversized that I had to get a special permit at every state I entered.) Fred's piece was the engine and it looked like the best piece, a far as tying down went.

We took off and headed up the freeway, but we only got about five miles along when the engine fell through Fred's trailer and started to drag on the road. We got stopped and put in a call to Caterpillar. They came out with a crane and lifted it up and when they did, they found that one corner of the motor had dragged on the road and would require extensive repairs. When we got that news, we decided I should go ahead, as it would be a week before Fred's load was ready to move again.

There is a big truck stop at Ontario, Oregon, which is situated at the foot of Cabbage Mountain, just off the freeway to the north. As I got to the off-ramp, I saw a sign that said, "Road Closed," so I went back to the truck stop and asked why the road was closed. The guy there said, "Because of the snow."

I said, "Snow? Where?" and he said, "It's snowing up top." I asked how much and I was told it didn't matter how much; I wouldn't be able to go, anyway, because I had an oversized load. I had to get a permit from the State Patrol Scales Office. Since this was on a holiday weekend, which included Friday, Saturday, Sunday and ½-day Monday, I would have to wait. I told him I already had a permit but he replied, "Not for inclement weather!"

I asked, "What weather?"

He said, "The snow." I looked outside and saw about two flakes of snow.

I waited and waited and waited again, all Friday and Saturday for the snow that never came. What did come were two other trucks with wide loads that had caught up to me. After waiting for what seemed like forever, I decided I was going to leave late Saturday, provided the snow continued to hold off.

At two a.m. Sunday morning, I told the other two guys that I was heading out and they agreed; it was time. There was no snow on the road and we were sick of waiting. We crept out onto the freeway as quietly as three oversized loaded trucks could. We started traveling and when we did we noticed that there were no service roads or off-ramps and that it was a limited access road. The only way on or off was at each end. We were about halfway through when we met a cop car coming toward us. When he saw us he put his lights on and because he couldn't get near us, we ignored him. We realized he could have radioed the other end and had a car standing by, but he obviously didn't as there was no one there and we breezed right through, with no snow!

Because it was Sunday, there was no permit office open and we made it through to Spokane. Now it did start to snow; the road to the Canadian border was snow-covered and it had no traffic. As we headed up there, would you believe it? I slid into a little ditch on the side of the road. We finally got a tow truck (Sundays are bad) and after breaking one cable, he got me back on the road again and we finally made it to the border. (It only cost me $50.) Crossing the border at Black Hawk, we were on the home stretch to Sparwood. Once we got rid of our loads, we headed down to Revelstoke and picked up a load of lumber for the Fraser/Surrey Docks.

The trip to Surrey was smooth and uneventful. When we arrived, we off-loaded and phoned dispatch. We were given loads to San Diego and then we were on the road again.

Chapter 15

Chicken and Dip

Fried Chicken

It was the middle of winter and Pat and I went empty to Chetwyn to pick up a bunch of drilling equipment, compressors, welders and various other bits of mining gear. After getting everything tied down using every chain we had, we headed for Vancouver. The road was extremely slippery and covered with black ice.

We neared the bottom of Pine Pass and as I rounded a right-hand corner, I hit a patch of pavement and ice. We slid off the road and there was nothing I could do except holler at my son to hang on. When the truck finally came to a stop, we were in a very deep ditch filled with snow. We were leaning so far over that the truck was on its side and when we climbed out, the wheels and tires made great seats, since they were perfectly level and about a foot above the road. Pat was able to get his butt into the wheel, while I sat on the tire and waited for an inspirational thought as to how we were going to get out of the ditch.

Suddenly, I remembered that the railway had a large bull-dozer, but that was about eight miles up the road. Now my problems included: How would I be able to get to that cat? Would the operator come down and help us? And anyway, would he be able to pull us out? Still sitting, waiting, we heard an awful roar coming from the road behind us. After a couple of minutes, an old truck loaded with chickens came around the corner and the driver stopped. We started to talk to him, but he held up his hand and I thought he was deaf. He hollered that the problem was his old beater had no muffler and on top of that he had no floor boards, so the noise was too loud to make out our words. After a few minutes of shouting back and forth, he offered me a ride to the top of the pass. Against my better judgment, I accepted the offer and told Pat to stay with the truck. When I climbed in, I had to find room for my feet around a cage of chickens and holes in the floor.

Once we took off, I think if I could have got the door open, I would have jumped out. Between the chickens squawking, the backfires and the flames and sparks from the exhaust that came in through the holes in the floor as we slid around corners, I went through hell! We finally reached the lodge and I stumbled out with my ears ringing, covered in chicken feathers and pretty sure I was on fire somewhere. I used sign language to thank the guy, then staggered over to the lodge and explained my situation to the guy with the cat.

He said that eight miles was a long way to take the cat down the road and it would cost me $100 a mile. I told him to go ahead, that was cheaper than a tow truck. We climbed up into the cat and away we went. It was a rougher ride, but at least there were no barbequed feather-covered chicken smells. When we got back to the truck, my son told me that someone from the highways department had stopped and warned him not to stay there as we were right in the path of a big avalanche and in his estimation, judging from the snow, he thought it was ready to let go anytime.

The guy with the cat backed into the ditch on the other side of the truck, hooked a cable on and tried to move the truck. No matter how much he tried, it would not move. All the time, he had his eye on the mountainside and he did not seem to put out much effort. Just then, another fellow showed up and, as it turned out, it was his cat. He climbed in, dug a huge hole, drove in and pulled the truck out. It took him about five minutes.

Once we got out, all the while checking the mountain, we went over the truck and the load. The truck had a broken headlight and a broken mirror. As far as the load went, we must have done a super job of tying it down—not one piece of equipment had moved. Neither of us got hurt in the slide, but I think I burnt holes in my pants; either that or those holes were from where the chickens had pecked them. From here on in, I think I'll take my chickens home fried!

Dam Load

One day in January, I was in the dispatch office and they came up with a load to Burns Lake, west of Vanderhoof. The load consisted of two boom boats, which are very small tugboats that are used to push logs around and make up the log-booms that are floated down the lake to the mill.

My daughter was out of school at the time so she asked if she could go with me and I said, "Sure, I'll pick you up later." My kids used to enjoy going on trips with me every chance they got and I liked the company. At times, they were even a help, folding tarps, picking up straps, etc. My loading spot that day was Annacis Island and after a great deal of messing around, because of the odd shape, I finally got both boats secure, went home to Surrey, picked Cathy up and we were off!

With such an unusually shaped load, I had to stop frequently and tighten chains and belts, so by the time we arrived at the job site (our destination), it was pitch dark. The foreman was there waiting and he insisted I unload that night. Normally, that would have been no problem, but he wanted me to unload on the other side of a 400-foot dam that was only 9 ½ feet wide, with nowhere to turn around at the other end. I had to back across with just my back-up lights. Cathy got out and watched from the road.

It took quite a while, since it was hard to see and really difficult to stay on the narrow strip of dirt. When I finally made it, it was a big relief. We unloaded with no trouble but as I headed back, I could see in my lights just how close I had come to going over the dam—there were spots all along where the edge of the road was broken away. Maybe it was a good thing that the lighting had been poor; I'd probably have never made it over if I'd really known how close I came to taking a dip into the dam!

When you're trucking, aim straight and pull from the hip;
If you don't you might falter and go for a dip.

Chapter 16

Punctures and Owies

Nails

Late one Saturday, I received a call to pick up a load of nails to go to Los Angeles. Because it was a rush load, I assumed it was loaded, ready to go. When I arrived at the plant it was about 7:30 p.m. and the trailer was sitting there, empty. The good news was the shipper was still there to load it. After loading and tarping, I went looking for a bathroom. The plant lights were out and I guess the shipper or watchman was sleeping.

I was wandering alone in the dark and I was not finding anything that looked like a washroom. Then I came to a cut-out, where they parked rail cars to load them. I could hardly see anything, but it looked about three feet down to the deck. I jumped down and I landed in a bucket of red-hot 2 ½ inch nails. I imagine they had been put there to cool off. When I landed in them, eight nails stuck into my left foot and seven in my right. As I fell out of the bucket (I had no choice, I couldn't step out or climb out—not with all the nails sticking in my feet!), I landed on my knees and had to crawl back to the truck.

I took my vice grips and pulled the nails out. It was tough, because some had gone right into the bone. After removing them, I wrapped the steps of the ladder with clothes and whatever else I could find to cushion them some so I could get up into the truck. By then, my feet had started to swell and I had to cut my boots off. One good thing about it was that the nails had been so red hot they cauterized the wounds and they didn't bleed.

Downing a handful of Tylenol, I decided I would continue on to Los Angeles, and hope the feet didn't get too bad. Handling the clutch wasn't too hard, because the position of the nail holes were in places where the pedal didn't hit. The brake and accelerator were a different story, but I started off with my sock-feet and by using the hand throttle and the trailer brake handle, it was bearable. I managed to get through customs with only a fair amount of difficulty.

Once I was out on the freeway, I pulled the throttle out and set it for 57 miles per hour; after that it was no feet required, for the driving, anyway. That didn't count the bathroom or food breaks. I got lucky there, though, courtesy of other drivers and take-out at truck stops. I would get on the CB, order what I wanted, and then when I got there, someone would bring it out—sometimes an employee of the truck stop or once in a while another trucker who I'd contacted on the radio.

When I arrived at the dock (on time, incidentally), I started to struggle out of the truck, but a longshoreman there told me to sit down. The guys there removed the tarp and tie downs and I did absolutely nothing as they unloaded the whole load. When they finished, they rolled the tarp up, loaded it on the truck and tied it down. Those guys made my day! My back haul was a load of pipe from Cloverdale, California, and the guys there were also just great. Even though I assured them I was feeling a little better, they did everything and were a huge help.

The trip back was fairly uneventful and since I could only hobble around, I got unloaded in Vancouver and took the rest of the day off. I headed for the hospital where they told me the wounds were healing fine, thanks to the cauterizing effect of those hot nails. All round, I was pretty lucky; being able to drive and finish my run and to get all that help. It was great!

"No act of kindness, no matter how small, is ever wasted."
– Aesop –

The Spike

I seem to have an affinity for nails. This is a story that illustrates how it only takes a second for something to jump out and grab you.

I was picking up a container at the CPR yard in downtown Vancouver. The yard had lots of piles of timber from railway crossings lying around. A bunch of us were walking between these piles of wood headed for the loading area and I hadn't even noticed that the crossings had large spikes sticking out of them. As I moved my left leg forward, I hit one of the spikes with my leg, just between my knee and my ankle. Those spikes were about a foot long and made out of 3/8-inch steel twisted into a corkscrew.

The spike went through my leg from front to back; the worst part was getting it out. I went to the hospital and they cleaned the wound out, filled it with sulfa, put in a rubber band and covered it up with a Band Aid. The nurse explained that the elastic was in there to allow the wound to heal from the inside out. Each time the dressing was changed the elastic would be pulled out a little further, until the healing was complete. They gave me some extra sulfa drug and Band Aids and told me I had to have it cleaned up every day, to stay off it, and to keep it elevated.

I had a load to Prince George and off I went. I made up my mind to go to the hospital as soon as I got there and get the cleaning done at Emergency, but when I made an appearance, they refused to do it. It needed to be done, so I took the Band-Aid off, pulled the elastic out and poured more sulfa into the hole. Then I put the elastic band back in with a toothpick. Each day of the week, I went through this same procedure and I pulled the elastic out a bit, turning my sleeper into an emergency room. It took about a week to accomplish the job, but finally the elastic was no longer a part of my wound; it was healed.

If you want a job done well, do it yourself.

Chapter 17

Rumbles and Rovers

Nature Calls: The Earthquake

My son and I were off to Chetwynd with a load of steel beams. It was a pretty routine run and when we arrived at our destination at eight a.m., we untied the load and the crane crew took over. They unloaded one beam out of the 12 that comprised the load, and then they sat. When I asked what was going on, I was told that the job had been "wobbled," or as a lay person would say, they were exerting strike action (working to rule) and could only unload two pieces a day. That means they would work four hours in the morning, unloading one beam, and four hours in the afternoon, during which the other beam would be unloaded, to be sure to get paid for the full day's work. They told me the reason they were "wobbling" the job was they were unhappy with the coffee.

After three days, they had unloaded six beams. By this time, I was getting choked with sitting around. I was just getting the basic standby time and I could have been out on another job! If they thought I was going to sit around for three more days because of a cup of coffee, they were nuts. That night, Pat and I got two crowbars and pried the beams off the truck.

The next morning the foreman came round and asked what the "&%*$#@" we did—how did those beams got unloaded? I told him I had no idea, except the bunkhouse shook like crazy and when we went out in the morning, the beams were on the ground. After a ten-minute "discussion," we were on our way, thanks to a very timely earthquake! Who says not?

Mount Shasta Rumble

This could have almost been another Nature story. The load I had was a mixed load for a sawmill that was just over the Oregon border, in California. It (the load) was a real horror story in that it was about as mixed up as possible, with steel, saw-blades, electrical parts, electric motors, cables, ropes—more stuff than you've ever seen. All the pieces had to be fastened down with chains, ropes, or belts. It ended up looking a little like a spider's web.

The first problems were at the customs office at the border. Everything had to have separate Bills of Lading and you can imagine what a mess that was. The next problem was keeping all of the stuff on the trailer: stopping to check the load, adjusting and tightening belts, chains and what have you. When I finally arrived at the mill, I wasn't allowed to untie or undo anything. Only electricians could unload electrical stuff, such as motors, pulleys, rolls of wire, etc.; the millwrights could only handle their stuff and the carpenters, theirs. It got really interesting when electric motors had gears on them; then the millwrights got right in there, arguing about who should unload what. The carpenters took off wood beams and plywood, etc. The parts that took the longest to unload were the steel angle iron pieces, since the only one allowed to touch them was the labourer who drove the forklift and he was home sick.

After a lot of rigmarole, all I had left on were 34 pieces of angle iron about 12 feet long. When I suggested I would take them off, that really got them going and wound right up! They were saying there was no way I could touch any part of the load, so I sat and waited for the labourer to show up. At ten a.m., the foreman came by and said the labourer was not coming in that day; he was still sick. When I asked what I was supposed to do he said, "You'll have to wait and see if he shows up tomorrow, or . . ." I broke in then, saying I had no food with me and he made a smart remark that this would be a good chance for me to lose some weight. It was then that I thought . . . maybe, because it's California, right? Just maybe there would be an earthquake and the stuff would fall off the truck. Would you believe it, right at noon, when everyone had left for lunch, that's exactly what happened?

I left a note for the foreman telling him that. That was an amazing thing that happened!

Aftershock!

The Hippy

Driving as a lease operator hauling general freight can be wild and wonderful due to the different types of load, the shape and weight, and the width and height. One of these over-wide and over-length loads was a rock drill I needed to move from Sparwood to the Cache Creek Machine Shop. The total length, including tractor, was 96 feet and the drill was 12 feet wide with odd pieces sticking out underneath. After driving to Sparwood to do the pickup, I had to stretch out a special trailer to 60 feet to accommodate the awkward load. While chaining the load down, I found a few pieces of steel welded onto the frame of the drill that projected down toward the road. They were on the rear corners and I knew I would have to watch them closely so they wouldn't catch on anything.

I decorated the whole consignment with red flags and wide load signs, picked up a pilot car as escort and we left for Cache Creek. There were lots of interesting spots to navigate: narrow and sharp corners and some pretty slender bridges. This was in the days of the hippies and they were to be found thumbing their way to unknown destinations everywhere along the road. As we approached a narrow section of the road with a bridge in the middle, we spotted a hippy at the near end of the bridge. He stood beside a duffle bag about three feet high that was right on the pavement. The pilot car stopped and my escort told the guy to move out of the way. He chose not to do so and accented his refusal with the raised finger salute.

The pilot car honked as I let go with horns and Jake brake and the guy finally moved, with more fingers . . . and as I nudged the rig over the bridge with little room to spare, and no possible way to move over, one of the pieces below the corner hit the duffel bag and it virtually exploded with dirty clothes flying everywhere—on the metal work of the bridge, on the load and all over the road!

The pilot car driver went back to check and all he found was clothes—no sign of the hippy and we searched for half an hour. I guess he thought we were after him because of all the finger messages, because he was nowhere to be found, so we carried on. Because of our low speed, when we arrived in Cache Creek, there were still underwear and T-shirts hanging on the load. For a long time after that, my truck was known as The Chinese Laundry.

Alaska by Harley

On my way back from a trip to Dawson Creek, I had to pick up a load in Prince George on Monday morning. This being Friday, I had lots of time, so I stopped that night and had a few hours of sleep. When I got up on Saturday, I was wandering back down the Hart Highway and as I came around a corner, there, in the middle of nowhere, a guy was pushing a motor-cycle up the road toward Dawson Creek. I stopped and asked what the problem was and he said his motorcycle would not start.

He apparently had camped out and the temperature got down to about 15 degrees and in the morning he couldn't get the bike going. I asked him where he was off to and he said, Alaska. I said, "Do you know how much snow they get up there?" and he said snow didn't bother him. I told him that I'd been up there a week earlier and Pink Mountain had eight inches of snow and I said that quite often it snows in October. I also mentioned that the nearest place in the direction he was headed was Dawson Creek, about 50 miles up the road. I sug-gested that he would be a lot better off going to Prince George and I could give him a lift. Since I had a low-bed trailer, it would be easy to load the bike on and take it back to a bike shop, where chances of getting it fixed were a lot better.

Finally, I talked him into it and we went to Prince George. We sat around over Saturday and Sunday, then I dropped him off at a bike shop and I went on my way. Before we split, we talked a lot and I found out he was a motorcycle cop in Long Beach. We exchanged phone numbers and addresses. After that, every time I went to L.A., I stopped and visited him. He was married with two kids. He used to come up and visit and go on trips with me in the truck.

One summer we even switched houses for a month, which made for a good holiday. He had a 1926 Model T and he used to let me use it for sightseeing when I was in Los Angeles.

I don't think he ever went to Alaska. He said when he left Prince George, he went through Banff and there was snow there, about four inches of it. He was quite pleased that I had talked him out of the far north trip.

I don't know what happened to him—we lost track of each other over the years—but I do know a motorcycle in Alaska, in the winter, would have been quite a sight!

Chapter 18

Work and Pay

Who's the Boss?

At one time I hired a young teenager to accompany me and help with the bull work and maintenance of the truck. He hadn't been with me long when we had a load that involved moving steel from Vancouver to Prince George. The weather had been lousy all day, with mixed rain and snow, and by the time we were loaded, it was mostly snow.

Heading out to the freeway, the weather turned worse and by the time we reached the truck stop at Flood (near Hope), it was chain-up time. I got everything set up and the chains were lying in readiness, but my helper had disappeared. I went ahead and chained up without a sign of him, anywhere. I was justifiably upset and just about at the end of my patience when he finally showed up. I asked him where the %$#@ he'd been. And he told me he had been helping a couple of young guys to chain up.

I spat out, "Well, I hope they paid you well, because I'm not going to. You were hired to help me. I hope they have room for you in their vehicle because you are fired!"

Good help is hard to find these days!

Getting Carded

Fuel prices had gone up quite a bit in B.C. and I was off on one of my many tips to California. I checked out the amount of fuel I had in the tanks and decided that fueling up in the States would save a bit of money. When I crossed the border, I kept a pretty close watch on the gas gauge and decided I could make it to a truck stop in Mt. Shasta. At that time, I was buying all my fuel with MasterCard and when I pulled into the truck stop I looked for the MasterCard Logo and saw it on the pumps and on the building, so I told the attendant to put in 100 gallons.

When he was finished pumping, I gave him my card and he said, "We don't take MasterCard." I asked what all the signs and decals meant then, and he told me that they had recently switched to Visa. At this point, because I was riled at their false advertising and also because of my being a stubborn SOB, I decided that I would only offer my MasterCard and the Diner's Club and Visa cards would be staying in my wallet. I gave the guy an ultimatum; it was MasterCard or he could pump the 100 gallons out of my truck. He argued that he would not do that and insisted I had to pay cash or something. When he further refused to run it through on his Visa machine, I told him to call his boss, and if he couldn't make a decision within the next 15 minutes, I was leaving. He said he was calling the police, and I said, "Go ahead!"

The State Patrol soon arrived and when he had heard all of the details and seen all of the MasterCard signs, he told the guy to either take my card or remove the fuel. The attendant refused to do either so the cop turned to me and said, "Do you have cash or another card?"

I answered with a white lie, strictly out of stubbornness, saying "I do not!"

He then turned to the attendant and asked him again to either take the card or pump out the fuel, but he said no to both options. The officer turned back to me and said, "On your way!"

I said "What?" He repeated it and added, "The next time you're by this way, if you feel obligated, stop and pay them." I said, "Sure, if they take MasterCard!"

Chapter 19

Close Quarters

Mad Moose

My son and I had a load of concrete beams for a dam 90 miles north of Revelstoke. This is the area that holds the record for snowfall in B.C. The record was eight feet (2.438 metres) overnight! There is so much snow at the mine site that they have yellow and red plastic poles hanging from the wires on the power poles so you'll steer clear of them, as the wires are reachable be anyone on foot. All the buildings are connected by tunnels and you have to be extremely careful, wherever you go.

The road had been plowed and the snow banks were about ten feet in height. As we started off, right behind another loaded truck, the snow on the road was about 18 inches deep, with huge banks on both sides. About 50 miles in, the guy in front stopped his truck dead. He was face to face with a bull moose, with no place to go. The moose couldn't climb out of the road and the truck could not get out of the way, so we talked on our radios trying to figure out what to do. We sat for about a half hour, trying to come up with a solution. His idea was to honk at it, mine was to go ahead real easy and maybe the moose would let itself be nudged over.

About this time, the driver's patience gave out and he leaned on his horn. As he did, the moose charged! All I could see was steam pouring out of his radiator and his brake lights going on. We got out and edged around his truck. The moose was out cold with one antler off and the other stuck through the rad. The other driver thought that if he backed up a ways and gave me enough room, I could get around him, go to the jobsite and send a tow truck back. He managed to back up and pull around the prone moose.

After much wriggling and positioning, and careful to keep our eyes on the moose at all times, we got by and got to the site. We found the tow truck and sent it back to the moose-ram site. We started to unload and were still at it when the tow truck returned with the truck and the moose in tow. The radiator and grill were a mess and probably cost the driver a pretty penny to get fixed. The tow truck driver thought the moose would be okay, so he planned to tow it on the snow and turn it loose when he got to an opening where it could get off the road.

Moral: Don't give Bullwinkle the horn!

Yellow Bird

Yellow Bird was the name of an Arrow driver who should have been known as Dodo Bird, as he was always making mistakes. One time in particular, we were hauling sluice gates from Prince George to Tri-Cities, Washington State. After we were loaded and I was tied down and ready to go, "Bird" was still trying to tie down his load with a huge chain (it was like an anchor chain for the Queen Mary) and he was hooking the chain to skinny little hooks meant for tying ropes. While we were travelling on our way to Tri-Cities, he had to stop several times and retie his load.

As we approached the on-ramp that went on the freeway to go to Richland, I turned right and he went straight ahead. I called him on the radio and told him he'd missed the off-ramp but he could carry on straight ahead and he'd get on in only two miles. He nearly had a fit! He then went ahead across the overpass and proceeded to take the off-ramp on the wrong side. Then he drove his truck the wrong way down the off-ramp, dragging his trailer over a concrete divider, tearing up a bunch of shrubs, bushes and concrete. As he got halfway around, he met two cars coming up and they both had to back down the ramp to get out of his way, since he was flashing his lights and blowing his horn.

I was parked on the other side of the freeway, trying to tell him on the CB that he was going to kill somebody. I let him know he was going the wrong way and there was a fence down the middle of the freeway and he couldn't get over to the right side anyway. He told me, "There must be a gate somewhere!" and I told him to turn around and take the off-ramp—it was only two miles. He said he was here now so he took off down the freeway, going the wrong way, looking for a gate and dodging cars.

As I watched in my mirrors, a half-mile down the road, I saw him cross over to my side of the road and I thought I must have misjudged the gate factor. He pulled in behind me and climbed out. As I was getting down from my cab I said, "You had to go quite a ways to find a gate, eh?" and as he was looking at the front of his truck, he said, "There was no gate." When I looked down I saw a bashed-up fender, a broken headlight and a bent bumper. He also had one bent wheel on the back and had lost one of his rolled-up traps. He had to walk across the freeway and up the ramp to carry it back. Then he said, "I made my own bloody gate!" It was one of many times that "Bird" wished he could fly.

Yellow Bird #2

I had the misfortune to have the Bird as a partner on a trip to the docks in San Diego. As you come to San Diego, right on the outskirts on I-5, there is a small rest area. I was following the Bird, headed for Pier 34, when he signalled a right turn, so I asked him on the radio where he was going and he said into the rest area to ask directions. I told him I knew where to go but he still pulled into the small rest area, and because it was so small, when he stopped his truck, my truck was left sitting out on the freeway in the midst of rush-hour traffic. I sat there for about ten minutes, waiting for either him to move or for me to hear the screech of brakes. I was lucky that all I heard were about 1,000 honking horns. I don't know how I was dumb enough to agree that he would lead off, but I did.

We had to go right downtown and through the central part of the commercial area of the city. There were Pier 34 signs with arrows all over the place. As we drove through, we came to a traffic light, Bird turned into the left-turn lane and stopped, jumped out of his truck and left it half in the turn lane with the back hanging out and with my truck blocking the other two lanes because I had been dumb enough to follow him. I thought we must have missed the signs to the pier. But no, I could see them; in and around the intersection were three signs for Pier 34. Bird had run across that intersection to ask for directions! I looked over just in time to see the guy he'd spoken to point at the Pier 34 signs and all the arrows.

When Bird finally got back to his truck, a very nice police-man gave us a couple of tickets. When he heard the story, he made Bird's ticket out for $250 and mine for $100. His, the cop explained, was for obstructing traffic and mine was for being dumb enough to follow him. It took the cop almost an hour to get the traffic sorted out. He sent us around the corner to wait. As I apologized, Stupid asked him how to get to Pier 34.

I sure didn't want to go on another trip with him. Now that I think of it, I don't remember seeing him again. Maybe they locked him up in his cage.

Patterson's Fiasco

One of my many loads for Arrow was hauling a large dump truck destined for Hawaii via ship from Oakland, California. There were two trucks hauling, mine and Ron Patterson's. I was fortunate to be running with someone who knew everything, and was never wrong about anything. These were very large trucks that hung over the trailers and called for wide load signs and when we got to Medford, Oregon, we had to remove the rear wheels and put them on the front of the trailer. These tires and wheels are about 400 pounds apiece and California weight restrictions stated they had to be on the front. I asked Ron how we were going to get the wheels up where we needed them and he said, "Don't worry, I know a guy in the tire shop at the truck stop in Medford and he's a friend of mine. He'll let us use the forklift."

When we arrived, "Mr. Wonderful" said that if I took the wheels off, he would be right back with the forklift. By the time he got back, without the forklift and with some story about how the guy couldn't do it,

There we were with 1,600 pounds of wheels and tires spread all over the parking lot and no forklift. After getting the guy's name, I walked back and talked to him. It turned out Ron had used the forklift before and beat the guy out of $30. I did about 20 minutes worth of talking and laid down $50, got the forklift and went back and loaded wheels and tires on my truck. As I was tying them down, Ron climbed on the forklift. I walked over to him and said, "No way, you are not supposed to use it!" He asked why not and I said, "Because you owe me $ 50." With a bunch of complaining, he paid me and I added, "Oh, yeah, when you take it back, you owe the tire guy $30."

I thought maybe the smart ass might have learned a lesson, but I was wrong. The California scales were a few miles down the road and as I pulled in, the Highway Patrol Officer stepped out to check my permits, wide load signs, tie downs, red flags, etc. The permits were picked up at a truck stop a couple of miles up the road. After the check, he waved me through. I pulled over and waited for "mouth" to come through. When he did, he pulled over behind the scales and parked. I walked over and asked what was wrong; he said he'd had an argument with the scale guy. Apparently the officer said Ron had made the permit out with the date backwards. That is, he had day, month and year, when it should be month, day, year. "Mouth" had said, "Bullshit!" and the scale guy said, "Park it, drop the trailer, bobtail (tractor only) three miles south, U-turn seven miles north. Go to the truck stop and get the permit filled out right. Then bring the loaded truck through the scales again."

Because there's no landing gear on low-bed trailers, Ron had to find rocks and junk to hold the trailer up. He finally did so and I had a nap while he was gone. Soon after I dozed off, the scale guy woke me up and asked if "mouth" was a friend of mine. I said, "No, why?" He said," He's going to be a while, so I thought maybe you wanted to leave," but I said I would wait; I needed a laugh. When Ron got back, he hooked up and pulled through the scale and once again parked where he had been and started to drop his trailer again. I asked what he was doing and he said, "That &^%$&@ is sending me back to the truck stop again; he says my wide load signs are too small."

Lesson: It pays to keep your mouth shut—at least don't argue with a cop.

You would think that the fiasco would stop there, but no. When we got to Oakland, I said, "Let's find someone to unload these things," and Mr. Know-it-all said, "I can do it." As soon as we put the wheels on, Ron jumped into the truck that was on his trailer and proceeded to rip half the suspension off when the right front wheel slipped off the trailer. After finding a large forklift and shelling out $70 per hour, he finally got it unloaded, then paid a longshoreman $30 to drive it. Mine cost me $20, as the guy was in a good mood.

So ends Patterson's Fiasco.

Chapter 20

Pool, Rocks, Dogs and Ice

Playing for the Table

This story is a little bit of a diversion from the usual trucking stories, in that it happened during a layover in Boise, Idaho. My eldest son, Mike, was with me on this trip from Vancouver to Spokane, Washington. Our back haul was a piece of mining equipment going from Boise to Sparwood, B.C. By the time we were unloaded in Spokane, we knew we wouldn't have time to get loaded with the back haul, as it was Friday afternoon. We just loafed our way to Boise and parked at a truck stop, had dinner and slept in the truck.

The next morning, we dropped the trailer and sort of cruised around as the town was new to both of us. We finally found a pub/café that looked okay, so we went in for brunch. The first thing we notice when we walked in was a pool table, and because it was early no one was playing so we played each other. Mike was a good shot; he used to play on a table in our basement and he'd had lots of practice. I used to play for a living; that is how I supported my family for some time.

After we'd played a couple of games, somebody put some money down and challenged us for the table, so we became partners. We ended up taking on all comers and played from about 10:30 a.m. until 11 p.m. We never lost a game; if we had played for money, not just the table, we would have done all right. At times there were up to 20 people lined up waiting, as there was a college right next door. I think every student in the whole institution was there.

Finally, after we had been playing for just over 12 hours, two young college girls took us on, beat the hell out of us and became local heroes, When they asked us where we learned to play like we did, we said Canada, like that was self-explanatory. On Monday, we loaded and came home. We were both pretty proud that we had played so well.

Glacier

One of our most memorable trips was hauling pipe for an exploratory oil well situated in the southern part of the Northwest Territories, almost into Alberta. After a long trip on the snow-covered Alaska Highway, we turned right onto a logging road just past Fort Nelson; our destination was 175 miles north. The road should have been called a trail; actually even trail is a little too flattering a description of this rugged bulldozer-built track. As we made our way toward our destination we came upon a small glacier, about 50 feet wide and part of the road that we had to cross. To get traction, we had to put our chains on to keep from sliding downhill; but we made it okay.

About a mile farther, we came to another patch of ice. The only difference was that this one was close to a half-mile across and ended in a lake at the bottom edge of the glacier; as near as we could estimate, about a half-mile straight down the ice mountain. We chained up everything, including the steering, axle and the trailer. We started out onto this sheet of ice very slowly and by the time the trailer made it onto the ice, it had swung over and almost directly below the tractor instead of behind it.

It was very scary as there was no road and only a few scraped-off spots that had been made by an earth mover being dragged across by two Cats, winches and a bunch of cable. All you could do in this situation was move at a crawl and hope your tire chains held up and your tractor didn't break down— or it could mean a sheer drop of the whole shebang into the icy waters of the lake.

Actually it was a very exciting half-mile trek, but the only thing going through our head was the knowledge that we had to do it all over again to get back home.

The Rock

One of the strangest loads I ever had was one rock. This rock had to be picked up in the northern Yukon, in the middle of nowhere; the only direction we were given was in mileage. When we got to the spot the mileage designated, there was nothing there except a giant boulder with a hole through it lying beside the road. At this point I still didn't know what it was. I sat and waited for a couple of hours, thinking someone might turn up with my load. I was glad, as I waited, that I had a low-bed trailer. This trailer is a lot stronger and can haul heavier loads. After I had looked all over the rock, I still had no idea what it was and what I was supposed to do with it. About this time, I heard a loud noise coming from the bush alongside of the road and a large bulldozer came into view. As it came closer, I could see a big smile on the operator's face. When he shut the Cat off, he said, "I'm sure glad to see you. We've got a boat to catch!"

I said, "What the hell is that rock and why do we have to catch a boat?"

The guy said, "That 'rock' is a 12-ton piece of jade that has to be on a boat to China in three days."

I asked him where it had come from and how it got to where it was now. He told me he found it in a riverbed 63 miles into the bush and got it here by drilling a hole through it and dragging it out with a Cat. It took him ten days to get it out of the river and out to the road; it took him 14 days to get a generator and the Cat in there. After he drilled the hole, he threaded a large cable through the hole and dragged it out with the Cat. [This is a brand-name for Caterpillar equipment, particularly the tractor] He then proceeded to build a ramp with the Cat and roll the boulder onto the trailer. Upon closer inspection, you could see the green colour all through it. With just that one hole in it, it took a long time to secure it. Three days later, it was on its way to China. It was an amazing Celestine (Celestite and Cellestial) Stone.

Killer

During my first marriage, my wife had expressed an interest in accompanying me on some trips to California. We had friends in Sacramento and Long Beach and we had been invited to stay over for a few days, whenever we wished. On this particular trip she and our terrier, Killer were along for the ride. All was fairly calm on the way down; the only problem was that the dog was having difficulties accepting the noise of the traffic and the shadows. Every time we went under an overpass, Killer had a fit! He couldn't stand the noise and he was frightened to death of any shadows.

Once the load was delivered, we were advised that we'd need to stay over for a couple of days to wait for a back-haul. The truck was a cab-over (for the uninformed, this type of truck is one in which the driver and passenger sit over the engine and access to the truck is by way of ladders built into the cab). Between the seats is a padded area, sort of a catch-all for papers, clothes, doggy treats, toilet paper, etc. In this case, it also held Killer; he'd kind of made it his home-away-from-home. Since he thought the shadows and noises were after him, whenever they appeared, he would run like a mad thing and make laps around the cab and sleeper; heaven help anyone who tried to hold him back! Still, my wife had insisted he come along and it was probably logical for him to make that padded section his home; after all, it's known as the dog-house. Besides, he had that name to live up to!

Things seemed to be going fine as we travelled along; the wife was driving and I was sitting in the driver's seat with my feet up on the dog-house. The next thing I knew, we drove under an overpass, and simultaneously my wife yelled, "Police" and the dog went nuts! He ran into the sleeper and around and around the walls, barking his head off. When he ran up the side of my head and launched himself toward the half-open window, I caught him by the leg as he was halfway out. I looked over toward my wife and she was barrelling over the doghouse toward the passenger seat, the dog and me! There I was, all but lost among the newspapers, dog biscuits, shoes, toilet paper, bills of lading and whatever and trying to get to the steering wheel that was unattended at this point. I managed to make it there at the expense of an elbow to the eye and a dog bite on the ass, and finally corralled the wheel. I guess the state trooper thought I was taking too long to come to a stop, so he hit the siren and the dog started howling like it was a small wolf! By the time I got the damned dog calmed down, the trooper was at the door of my cab; I'm not sure whether he had his gun unsnapped, or not.

He asked me for my papers and by the time I located my log book, registration, bill of lading and Driver's License, and he'd had time to take in my bare feet, he was looking at me and the situation very strangely! Then the dog started to bark through the narrow opening of the window and the officer asked, "What were you doing in the truck?" I explained about the dog and the shadows and noises, the barking and especially the siren. Meanwhile, he checked over my log book, then turned to me and suggested, "You should lock the dog up somewhere. Oh, incidentally, what were you trying to throw out the window before you stopped?"

I said, "It was my wife, not throwing anything but catching hold of the dog to stop him going out the window!"

His response to that was, "Maybe you should have helped him!" I told him he was probably right!

Nothing was said about who was driving and there was no indication that he was aware we had switched seats; but I sure didn't have any idea why or what had happened in those few moments of a truck gone wild. My wife's explanation was that she panicked when she saw the policeman because she thought it was illegal in the U.S. to drive with a learner's permit.

This adventure marked Killer's last truck ride!

Chapter 21

Long Odds

The Long, Long Haul

I was probably only a teenager when the movie *A Long, Long, Trailer* came out, starring Lucille Ball and Desi Arnez, but seeing a rerun of that show years later reminded me of a trip I'd lived through and wasn't anxious to relive, any time soon.

When I checked in at the dispatch office one morning, I was told to come to the yard and pick up the log bunks and a steer trailer with bunks on it for a load of 90-foot poles to go to Chetwynd, B.C. A short while later, I arrived at the yard, rounded up my rear driver, a guy named Bob, and all the equipment. I had my son, Pat, with me and we headed down to Annacis Island to get loaded. Once we were loaded, we still had our work cut out for us. We needed to come up with a map and plan to get us to the freeway quickly, since there were restrictions on the over-long load for daylight driving only. We needed to get over the Port Mann Bridge by four p.m. and thankfully, we managed to squeak through. Without our pilot cars, we never would have made it.

We arrived in Flood (near Hope) just as it was getting dark, so we opted to stay overnight. I wouldn't have wanted to make that trip at night! Anyway, Pat was designated as the navigator and radio operator, telling Bob which way the corners went so he could steer through, because he could see nothing from his steering position under the load.

The next morning, we set out and went right down the main street of Hope to the Fraser Canyon, travelling through lots of corners and bridge approaches. At times, the pilot car had to stop traffic altogether so that we could have room to get through. Even then, some cars tried to pass us to get through ahead of us. One of the roughest parts that day was just past the top of Jackass Mountain, where there are a couple of really sharp corners. If you missed them, the drop there was roughly 600 feet into the Fraser River. Another bad area was the strip between Boston Bar and Spence's Bridge; even with Bob steering, it was pretty spooky on some of those corners. Just past Yale, we came to the tunnels. The shorter tunnels were not too bad; we only had to stop traffic on both sides and then we got through with room to spare. Alexandria Tunnel was a different story! The tunnel is long (about a half-mile long) and it curves. I was pretty tense until I realized that we were going to make it through okay.

After the tunnels, everything went smoothly except for the odd idiot who passed, or tried to, when they had no way of even seeing if cars were coming in the other direction. Our next challenge was at Quesnel, where there were difficulties first getting over the bridge and then with overlapping traffic lights. After Quesnel, things were looking pretty good until the bypass at Prince George. They had their stoplights set so you had about 20 seconds on green. There was no way a truck and a long, long load would be able to get through the light in 20 seconds. We tried and we didn't make it. The police were lying in wait for trucks that tried and failed. We received our ticket, but later disputed it on those grounds and we had the citation rescinded.

The remainder of the trip was a little hairy as well, because we were travelling Hart Highway, with no shoulders. That keeps you alert but on edge all the way. The same thing happened at Pine Pass, N.W.T., where it's not only narrow but pretty rough. We were lucky enough to make it all the way, but not without some close calls, especially one in which some bright spark drove right under the load to get ahead and ended up on the wrong side of the road, waiting for hours for an opening in traffic. I guess, though, it all goes with the territory. Bob and Pat did a fine job and just like Desi and Lucy (in the movie, that is), we all lived happily ever after.

Odd Job

The more I write and recall all the different loads I've hauled to all the unusual places, the more it seems to stimulate my old memory and all of a sudden, out pops another oddity, tale or recollection. In this case it was a load of concrete main beams 80 feet long for a bridge in the interior of B.C. Four of the beams weighed about 50,000 pounds each, which meant only two to a load.

The way they were loaded was unusual in that normally, a steer trailer would be used, but since they were all in use somewhere else, we had to improvise. Besides being 80 feet long, the beams were nine feet wide and four feet deep. We started off with a log bunk sitting on the fifth wheel. This is a heavy piece of metal that pivots when the tractor turns and one end of the beam was securely chained to the bunk that is fastened where a trailer was normally located. The back of the beam was lifted up and a flat-deck trailer was put under the back 45 feet of the beam and the front of the trailer was chained to the beam, which held it in place. With the trailer holding the back up and chained down, that left about 35 feet of the beam acting as the backbone of the trailer.

After we ran our electrical and air lines and hung our long load signs, we had about the weirdest looking set of loads I had ever seen. With the pilot cars, it made quite a unique train: four trucks with long distances between the front and back wheels. It was very challenging trying to keep the rear wheels in your own lane on some of the corners. We were off, though, and on our way north of Kamloops, about 50 miles toward Clearwater and roughly 385 miles north of Vancouver.

When we arrived, we were all surprised that not one of us had had a problem. We kind of jumped to conclusions as to where the beams were to be off-loaded. They had dug a trench into the riverbank and out into the river, so we could be as close to the footings as possible. As we started to back down, because of the angle of the trench, the landing gear of the trailer caught on the gravel and we had to use the crane to lift the back of the load until the legs were clear. Once we were unloaded, the crane was used to remove the bunks and then it was okay to hook up the trailer, load our gear and head for home, with another off one under our belts and ready for the books.

Chapter 22

Closed Crates and Duct Tape

Crossing the Border

If you've been reading this book you may remember the story about the Bear Mine and the multi-million dollar loads that had to be treated with kid gloves. On this load, the crates were made of 12 by 12 timbers bolted right through the trailers. The insides were all lined with foam rubber; then each piece to be shipped was lowered into its crate. Then it was belted down and wrapped in more rubber. Next the top was closed with more 12 by 12s. The trip was fairly uneventful, except that the owner's instructions stipulated that our speed on the gravel road was to be slow enough to keep it smooth: five miles an hour!

When we finally arrived at Sumas Customs, all our papers were in order and a customs officer came out to look at the load. He had the nerve to say, "Open them up!"

I said, "There's no way that they will be opened," but he repeated, "Open them up." I told him to get his superintendent out there because they weren't going to be opened up. The superintendent showed up and asked what was going on. I explained. He went and had a look at the loads and the papers. By this time I'm beginning to get a little hot.

The superintendent walked over to the border guard and said, "If you want them opened, go and get your chain saw and your cutting torch and open them up. When you have inspected both of them, close them again, seal the holes and if there's any damage, it will be your responsibility." Then he added "Either get started or get back to work; and you two drivers have five minutes to get out of here!" We did!

If at First You don't Succeed — Try Duct Tape

Some loads can be a never-ending source of frustration. I was given one such load: an earth-moving shovel that was already loaded on a low-bed trailer out near the Bowron Lakes, out of Prince George. We finally found it sitting on the side of a gravel road in a swamp. It was on the trailer, alright; the only problem was the load had been left in a wet, muddy area and it had sunk into the mud so far that the blocks holding up the front had disappeared under the water. When we backed up to hook up to the trailer, it was about eight inches too low and the 5th wheel would not even go under the front of it. It was quite a dilemma as all we could do was to try to jack it up.

The ground was wet and soggy; we were going to have to dig it out and it kept filling up with water. We couldn't find anything to brace up the jack to keep it from sinking. We looked everywhere and finally found a piece of steel floorboard from out of the shovel; took the bolts off and set down in the mud. That gave us about six inches on the one side and we tried again, but it still wasn't high enough. I backed the truck up to the front of the trailer and it still wouldn't work.

Getting a little desperate now, I looked at the engine in the shovel we were going to move and after about an hour I got it going. Moving the truck again, I dug down in front of the trailer with the shovel and managed to scrape some gravel off the road, building up the gravel over the mud until I managed to get hooked up. Still, the lift I'd built was so fragile I had to use the shovel to get more gravel to go under the truck. After about four hours, we got the trailer out. The plate from the floor of the shovel was not so easily recovered. It stayed— and is probably still buried there.

In this business, almost every load has its own set of problems, but at least it is seldom boring. The rest of the trip to Hope was non-eventful but then, after all the work involved in hooking up, maybe anything else would seem like nothing. All in all, it was a huge relief to drop our load and move on.

Chapter 23

Truck Parts

Fire Truck

Pat and I had a load of hardware for Cominco, in Trail, B.C. The trip up went well and after we unloaded in Trail the dispatcher sent us to Nelson to pick up a load of lumber for the Surrey-Fraser docks. Once we were loaded and tied down, I discovered a flat tire on the trailer. With a great deal of searching, we managed to find a tire place and while the guy fixed the flat, we went for something to eat. When we finished, we went back and found that the tire job was done, so we squared up with him and took off.

By this time, a light rain had started and just as we got to Christina Lake hill, it turned to fog. The hill was very steep and pretty much fogged in. We started down and visibility was very poor. I could not see anything in my mirror but fog. As it turned out, that fog was actually smoke! The tire we had repaired had gone flat and caught on fire! The brakes had generated so much heat that the tires were all burning now and so was the deck and the load of lumber. When we got to the bottom of the hill, everything was on fire!

We'd just passed the Christina Lake Volunteer Fire Department, so I sent my son back to get a fire truck. Meanwhile, I pulled over and backed into a three-foot snow drift. I jumped out and threw buckets of snow on the tires, the load and the trailer. As the fire truck pulled up, I had just got the flames out. The fire truck didn't have a thing to do and I dragged the trailer to an empty lot beside a gas station. My son and I had to sit there for three days, waiting for tires from Vancouver to get loaded on another truck and get up to Nelson; then we had to mount the tires, etc.

On the second day, a guy from the Fire Hall came over and wanted to know when I was going to pay my bill. I said, "What bill?" and he said I owed them $800 for putting out the fire. I told him that his fire department did not put one drop of water on the fire and even if they had, $800 was way too much. I added that I was not interested in buying his fire truck. As it turned out, Arrow paid it and charged it back to me. When they gave me the invoice, I asked where my fire truck was!

Cables and Chains

My son and I were hauling three empty flat-deck trailers from Chetwynd to North Vancouver. We had done the same thing before and the yard guys in North Van had gone on and on about the chains not being tight enough, so I told Pat to find a four or five-foot length of 2 ½ inch pipe. When he came back with the pipe, we put six lengths of chains over the trailers and three lengths of cable. We were pretty hefty guys; at that time I weighed about 300 pounds and my son was about 240 pounds We started with the cables and a bar with a pipe extension; we got the cables just as tight as we could. Next we used the chains and we got them so tight that when you hit them with a pipe, they sang; now, that is really tight. We tried to undo them and we couldn't. We checked on the way back and there was no slack in them at all. When we arrived in North Van we dropped the trailers in the yard, picked up another load and left.

The next day I got a message from the dispatcher, wanting to know what we did with the cables and chains. I told him that the yard guys had said the load before was almost loose, so we made super-sure they were tight this time, why? He said they were so tight they had to cut them off with a cutting torch. I said, "We were following orders!"

Moral: Watch what you ask for.

Chapter 24

Smoking It!

The Drag Race

The last truck I bought was a Kenworth cab-over with a double bunk. This tractor was equipped with a 450 Cummins Diesel and an Allison 5-speed automatic transmission. When this truck took off, there was not a tractor that could keep pace with it. The transmission shifted so smoothly, it was away ahead of everyone else.

We were hauling ore from Faro to Whitehorse and working for White Pass and Yukon Trucking Services. We were actually filling in for a bunch of broken-down White Pass trucks. Arrow agreed to sublease some of their trucks to help them out. It was a tough run and our trucks did not look so good either—they were always dirty and had broken windows, etc.

My son and I were sitting in the beer parlour of the Whitehorse Hotel. At the next table were a bunch of cowboys; the local Kenworth dealer had picked them up at the airport in a brand-new Kenworth with a 600 HP motor. They were all sitting around talking about what a great truck this was and saying that there was no truck that could come close to beating it in a race.

My son asked what type of transmission it had in it and the driver said 15-speed. Pat then asked if the guy wanted to race. The guy asked what kind of motor we had and I answered that it was a 450 Cummins. The guy was so greedy and confident that he forgot to ask about the transmission. I asked him what he wanted to race for and he said, "How does $500 sound?" I told him that was fine and to get someone neutral to hold the money. He said Dave would hold it, if that was okay with me. He then introduced me to the other guys at the table: Dave, a singer, and three guys from his band. They were there to put on a show the next night in downtown Whitehorse. I said, "Keep your eyes open tonight and you'll see a show."

Due to the fact that the bar was open all night, we decided to race five blocks down the main street right away. Dave held the money and he was to be the starter, too. After we got all lined up he dropped his neckerchief and we were off! You could hear the 600 roaring away as he took off in 1st and 2nd gears. By the time he got up to 3rd, he was about 200 feet in front of us and I hadn't even started, yet.

My son said, "Are you going to go?"

I said, "Do you think he has enough of a start?" I heard a "yep" so I said, "Why not?" All of his buddies were laughing and cheering until I put my foot down. I passed him when he had made about a block and a half, already in 3rd gear and going away! I finished the five-block race two blocks ahead of him and passed him on my way back.

When I got back to the start line, I collected the money and bought a few rounds as I explained all about my truck. I suggested to the other driver, if he was ever going to do it again, to be sure and ask about the transmission. This wasn't much of a Drag Race.

Smoking Tires

We were hauling a load of parts for a very large earthmover that was going to Whitehorse. I had a new truck and an old low-bed trailer. The new truck had a unique braking system called a transmission retarder. It used the oil in the transmission to act as a brake . . . Well, it was supposed to, but instead of stopping, it heated up. When it did, the brakes worked at about half of their capability. I managed by using the truck and the trailer brakes—which called for a bit of finesse and a lot of caution because if they get hot, they fade and you end up with no brakes at all. The system it should have had is known as a Jake brake: when the Jake is applied, it turns the engine into an air compressor, which works really well.

As we progressed up the Alaska Highway and the hills got steeper, the brakes were less and less efficient. We finally got to Steamboat Mountain, which is a very steep hill. As we started down the hill, I tried to keep it slow and not let it get too warm, but about halfway down, everything started to heat up and the brakes started to fade. If there had been a runaway lane anywhere near, I would have taken it!

There was about a half-mile more hill and about 100 feet of brake left. The brakes were all smoking and squealing. I made it around the last corner doing 40, tops! As I crawled along at five mph, trying to cool everything down, my son climbed out to look at the tires and just as he did, two of them blew! It almost took his ears off; he couldn't hear for a week and even at that, he was very lucky. He could have been killed. The next week, the truck was sporting a new Jake brake, and was lots safer.

Judgment Day (Almost)

My son and I picked up a large asphalt tank from Chetwynd to go to Surrey. The tank was part of a paving plant and measured

50 by 10 by 10 feet. It only had two large tires on it about three feet high and a foot wide. I didn't care for the fact it only had the two tires as this was dangerous. We left Chetwynd and though I was taking it real easy, as we went around a small right-hand corner the left-hand tire on the trailer blew. I became super busy trying to keep the trailer upright, because if it went over, the truck would go over, too.

As I was fighting to stay upright, I heard a loud clanging noise in the bush to my left. The tires on the trailer had lock rings on them: metal rings to hold the tire on. These rings weighed 10 to 15 pounds apiece and when the tire blew, the ring came off and flew into the bush. The noise I had heard was the ring hitting a rock and ricocheting out of the bush. When it came out, it was moving so fast you could hardly see it. It flew at the truck and narrowly missed coming straight in the window. It passed right in front of the windshield. If it had come in the window, it would have taken care of both of us.

When I finally got the rig stopped and it stayed upright, both of us were shaking like leaves. Once we calmed down, I phoned Arrow and after I informed them I wouldn't pull that tank without new tires on it, they sent two new tires. After I phoned in, we went looking for the flying ring and we found it close to the road.

Almost too close!

The Replacement Truck

One of the times my truck broke down and was in the shop for a couple of days, the company I leased from asked me to drive one of their local tractors. I was to pick up a container in Seattle. The truck they gave me to drive was a cab-over with no sleeper, a very small truck. Because it was a town tractor and was often hooked up to all kinds of different trailers, it came equipped with two ramps welded to the back end of the frame.

This allows the tractor to back under very low trailers, since the ramps are closer to the ground.

For me, with my extra–super-sized frame, driving down to Seattle in this vehicle was like riding in a phone booth. I finally made it and loaded a 40-foot container that had 5,200 TV picture tubes in it. When I arrived at customs, I had to drop the trailer, as it was Friday evening and the customs broker was closed. I left the trailer and took the tractor back to the yard, then went home. Early on Monday I picked up the tractor and hooked up to trailer and went to the brokers. Once I had received all the paperwork, I left for the yard.

Soon, I found myself at the junction of Pacific Highway and 8th Avenue. I slowed for on-coming traffic and started a left turn, but as I proceeded into the corner, the left side of the tractor and trailer lifted up and kept on going until it landed on its right side. When it came down, a telephone pole was sitting six inches behind the cab. It had landed very softly and all I could see in my mind was a picture of 5,200 broken TV picture tubes.

Another driver came over to discuss the occurrence, since he had been travelling right behind me. He said I was doing about five miles an hour and the trailer rolled, almost gently, sort of in slow motion. He said he had never seen anything like it; the whole thing just lifted up and kept going. I never got hurt at all and when they checked, only one picture tube was broken.

Once I had done some checking and looking around, I figured out what had happened. When I had gone back to the yard on Friday night, someone else had needed to use the tractor over the weekend and moved the 5th wheel forward, much farther ahead. The ramps on the frame were pushed back far enough that they caught on the undercarriage of the trailer when I started into the slow turn. When they caught, it turned the tractor and trailer into one piece, with no turning point in between. The "tandem" rig wasn't able to turn the corner, so it simply rolled. You can only imagine how softly it landed if it only broke one tube out of the 5,200 potential breakers.

Definitely, a Lucky Break!

Chapter 25

Golden Balls

Oh, Balls!

One of the odd loads that we hauled to a mine up on Lac La Biche, near Gran Isle, was grinding balls (these are used to mix with the ore in a mixer which is then rotated at a high rate of speed so the heavy grinding balls smash the ore into small pieces). To ship the balls, we used ordinary trailers with no sides on them; we put pipes in the holes and two-by-ten planks to make sides. After we got the planks in place, we fastened them down with chains and spikes.

I got loaded with a full load of balls, checked that it was tied down properly and away I went, up the Fraser Canyon Highway. I stopped a couple of times on my way, to check on the load and it was okay. About two miles before Cache Creek, there used to be a truck stop called "Boston Flats." The truck stop was about ten feet below the road and on a bit of a left-hand curve. As I was going by, I looked in the right hand mirror and saw sparks flying. When I stopped, I discovered one of the planks had bounced up and had a ball wedged under it, and I had lost about a quarter of my load. Since I had to pay $800 deductible for any losses, I was a little choked!

About this time, two trucks stopped beside me: a pick-up and a semi. The pick-up belonged to the guy who owned "Boston Flats," and apparently several grinding balls had laid waste to his truck stop and his café. It cost me $500 for a broken fuel pump (the balls took the top right off it) as well as a broken window and door in the coffee shop. Fortunately they didn't hit anyone. The guy in the semi said there was a big pile of balls at the bottom of Oregon Jack, which is a local hill about ten miles west of Boston Flats.

After I reclaimed by $500 worth of missiles (seven of them), I started to think about the rest of the run-away load. Since I'd already shelled out $500, the $800 more was not too appealing a prospect, so I decided to go back to Oregon Jack and see how big the pile was. When I got back, balls were all over the corner. I decided that I would get as many as I could and maybe add some rocks or snow or something. I stared to pick them up and they were heavy little things, about the size of baseballs and about six pounds each in weight. After dropping one on my toe, I began to wonder how smart this was, so I tried a different approach. I tied the sleeves of my Indian sweater together and filled it with balls, and then carried it onto the trailer. After a few tons, several limping miles and many hours, I finally gave it up and, hoping I could get away with it, I took off after doubling up on my chains and ropes.

When I arrived at Lac La Biche and our destination at Gran Isle in a blizzard, I had to back onto a barge. It's bad enough in the daylight; but at night, all you have is your back-up lights and as I backed onto the barge it sank about two feet and I thought I'd gone into the lake. I made it though, and when I got to the other side, I drove onto the scales. Somehow I was within the minimum load and had successfully brought the load, 'er, the . . Balls to them!

Bad Luck

Pat and I were hauling chlorine from Tacoma to McKenzie. Anyone who doesn't know what this is, it is an extremely caustic gas that is used for bleaching woodchips in pulp mills. It is the same gas used in World War One. It's not only toxic— if it gets into the air intakes on trucks, it will burn the interior out of the engine.

When we were at the mill, waiting to unload, there was one truck in front of us and one railway car. When they unload the truck, they park it inside the building. The railway car is parked outside and the gas gets pumped out of the railway car through a large hose. When it came time to move the tank car, somebody forgot to remove (unhook) the hose. When they moved the tank, the hose broke and about 50,000 gallons of chlorine started to spread around the yard. Since it moves along the ground, it means you better start dodging the green gas and staying as far away as possible. Fortunately, we were far enough away that I had time to move my truck.

The other driver jumped out of his truck and took off as the cloud enveloped his whole truck, but the gas moved faster than he could run. In the meantime, the gas got to his truck and was sucked into the air cleaner and completely ruined his engine. The cloud moved so fast it caught the other driver when he tripped and when we got to there to help, he was clear of the gas, but he was coughing and choking as we dragged him to the First Aid building. After they checked him out, they shipped him out to Prince George. I heard later he had some bad burns, but he was okay.

That's a bit of good luck.

Loads of Gold – Another Story

In one of my earlier tales, I spoke of loads of gold, saying it was another story. Well, this is it! My son, Pat, and I had a load to Stewart and a backhaul from Fredrick's Gold Mine near Cassiar. When we arrived, my son asked me if it was okay for him to see about a job working for the mine, as he'd heard they needed a truck driver. He also mentioned they paid four times what I was paying him;. I told him to go for it and make himself some money.

When I found out what my backhaul was, I nearly flipped! It was a four-by-four box of unrefined gold! The load was destined for Vancouver and after it was all loaded and tarped, I got another surprise. A fellow named Rob was to ride with me as an armed guard, like in the olden days, riding shotgun on a gold-laden stagecoach. The whole scenario made me quite nervous.

Fortunately, the whole trip went well and Bob never had to use his shotgun once. There were no gangs of bad guys laying in ambush anywhere and when we arrived in Vancouver, we unloaded at Brinks under a whole lot more security. I never did find out the actual value of that load, but with all that security, I'm betting it was a goodly amount!

Incidentally, Pat only lasted three weeks at his lucrative job; he got homesick and quit.

FINALLY THERE

We're There

The years have passed too quickly
The time has gone too fast
I expected that time would stand still for me
That my buddies and trucking would live to the last
But I hung up my "ears" quite a while ago
I parked the old girl way out back
"The Fugitive" retired; I gave up the open road
I miss trucking every day and wish I could haul one more load
To Whitehorse or to San Diego
Now where the hell did yesterday go?
I've loved that I relived a few of my trips
And wrote it down before I threw in my chips
As I sit reminiscing in my custom wheelchair
I know we started off right HERE and
now we've come to THERE

Glossary

Beaver biscuits	Lumber load
Bed-Bugger	Furniture hauler
Binders	Brakes
Blankets	Tarps
Boots	Tires
Bubble gum machine	Radar
County Mounty	Local law enforcement
Doghouse 1	Area over the motor in the cab
Doghouse 2	Trucker's residence when you're in deep kaka at home
Ears	CB Radio
Good Buddy	Stranger on the CB
Handle	Name (Nickname)
House	Cab
Kenworth Clamp	Coat hanger
Kenworth Wrench	Large hammer
Landing Gear	Legs under the trailer

Load of Muffins or Hauling Postholes	Running empty
Load of Potato Chips	Nearly empty load
Load of toothpicks	Truck hauling logs
Long hauler	Cross-country driver (Highway driver)
Long nose	Conventional truck with a hood
Lot lizards	Truck stop "ladies of the night"
Machinery Trailer	No ramp
Maintenance Magic	Duct tape
Ten four	Okay. Got it! Roger
Take a ten-ten	Heed the call of nature
Ten-seven	Lunch break

Printed in Canada